Praise for *More Than a Minute*

"**More Than a Minute** provides a guide for doing the right things well in today's world of hyper everything. Spend the time to read this one. It will make a difference in how you lead and manage your business."

—John Bell, CEO, Total Training, Inc.

"Holly is able to offer a unique perspective that is gained from years of successful business leadership experiences. This translates into constantly evolving approaches related to improving organizational effectiveness. Her tools work in today's environments of constant change and increasing complexity."

—Sid Ferrales, Senior Vice President,
RealNetworks, Inc.

"What a refreshing look at how the basics of leading and managing have evolved. In this book, Holly does an excellent job of giving leaders and managers the tools they need for today."

—Vikki Loving, Founder & CEO,
InterSource Recruiting, Inc.

"A must read for any leader or manager today as well as for those wanting to be one. I only wish I had it twenty years ago!"

—Connie Parker, Managing Partner, J.E.
Robert Companies

"**More Than a Minute** has become my *go to* guide for making my businesses more successful. Simple and right on target for leading and managing today."

—Kirke Curtis, CEO, Pamet Systems and successful serial entrepreneur

"Holly has created a valuable resource for today's leaders and managers to figure out what needs to get done and how to do it well."

—Pat Gallagher, Director, Learning & Development, Thomson Reuters

MORE THAN *a* MINUTE

How to Be an Effective Leader and
Manager in Today's Changing World

Holly G. Green

CAREER
PRESS

Franklin Lakes, NJ

MORE THAN A MINUTE
EDITED BY KRISTEN PARKES
TYPESET BY EILEEN DOW MUNSON
Cover design by Rob Johnson / Johnson Design
Printed in the U.S.A. by Book-mart Press

To order this title, please call toll-free 1-800-CAREER-1 (NJ and Canada: 201-848-0310) to order using VISA or MasterCard, or for further information on books from Career Press.

CAREER PRESS

The Career Press, Inc., 3 Tice Road, PO Box 687,
Franklin Lakes, NJ 07417
www.careerpress.com

Library of Congress Cataloging-in-Publication Data
Green, Holly G. 1963–
    More than a minute : how to be an effective leader and manager in today's changing world / by Holly G. Green.
        p. cm.
    Includes bibliographical references and index.
    ISBN 978-1-60163-033-9
        1. Management. 2. Leadership. 3. Strategic planning.
    4. Communication in organizations. I. Title.

HD31.G747 2009
658.4'092--dc22

2008021175

For Mark,
Brett, and
Claire,
who create my context of excellence.

><

Acknowledgments ▶

There are many people to thank and not enough pages to list them all. For all of you who encouraged, cajoled, and nagged me into writing this book, a heartfelt thank you! Thanks to all my victims, I mean clients, who have trusted in me to help them achieve even greater success, and for allowing me to use your stories as a way to help others.

A special note of appreciation goes to my researchers, Jessica Kole and Kristen Long, as well as my content development assistant, Christine Messier. Your patience, persistence, and dedication were instrumental in pulling it all together.

It has been a fun journey and one filled with learning and unlearning along the way. I deeply appreciate the opportunity to share this material with you, and look forward to hearing about your success in using it!

Contents

Preface

The leader or manager of 25 years ago, now long retired, recalls fondly how he taught his reports, and they taught their reports, constantly adapting and improving upon what they learned. My how some things changed over the years....

In the past 25 years the world of work has changed dramatically in many ways. Computers sit atop almost every desk and e-mail is a common communication vehicle today, though neither existed in the traditional workplace a few decades ago. Video conferencing, the Internet, and intranets, along with the convenience of mobile phones and PDAs provide a platform for connecting, deciding, and implementing decisions in time frames we could not have imagined a few years ago. The workforce is much more diverse, and global boundaries are often blurred.

Compounding these realities is the fact that there are now four generations at work in the U.S. workforce and three generations in most other countries. People are living longer, and the time span between generations is getting shorter. Employees are staying in their jobs longer or re-entering the workforce after traditional retirement age. A significant labor shortage is forecasted for 2010. Each of the four generations has very different attitudes, communication styles, motivation, and expectations of work. They also have different values and different ways of getting things done. For purposes of this book, we have used the following general parameters when we refer to the four generations:

Generation	Years born
Traditionalists	before 1945
Baby Boomers	1946–1964
Generation X	1962–1980
Millennials	1981–2000

There is an overlap with some of the Baby Boomers and Generation Xers. These employees are often referred to as Tweeners—they have characteristics of both generations depending on where the strongest influences came from during their early years.

Keep in mind that much of what is outlined in the following chapters applies across all employees: strategic planning with individual goal-setting and feedback, including encouragement and constructive guidance, are still solid management practices that can be used effectively in today's world. However, the way they look, the process for achieving them, and the environments they are applied in look very different today. Unfortunately, the pace of work today creates a context where many leaders and managers believe they have to establish and perform complicated and convoluted activities to keep up. They have lost sight of the power of the basics and have become consumed with seemingly urgent tasks that keep them spinning in circles, going nowhere.

When employees are asked, it is their leader or direct manager that most affects their productivity and performance in the workplace. Employee surveys indicate areas related directly to management, such as the following, are most often rated the lowest.

- ❧ My manager provides me the tools and resources to do my job well.

- ❧ I regularly receive praise or recognition from my manager for a job well done.

- ❧ The person I report to cares about me as a person.

- ❧ Management does an effective job of telling employees about my company's plans and developments.

- ❧ My manager provides me with a clear sense of direction (goals and instructions).

- ❧ My manager fully understands my job demands.

In my work with companies of all shapes and sizes around the globe, I have seen examples of great leaders and managers. The ones that stand out are those that do the basics well. They focus energy on getting the right foundation built, and they know how to apply the right tools at the right time to make a real difference. They make certain employees know and believe in the goals. They communicate consistently and with clarity. They provide feedback, recognition, and opportunities for others to learn and develop. They also focus on their own constant learning. In the end, these are the leaders and managers that achieve more and experience much greater success than those that become consumed busily engaging in nonproductive activities.

It is no longer enough to talk about being a good leader or manager; today **you have to be a great leader or manager**!

This book was written to support leaders and managers in focusing their energies. It is a simple reference guide to assist you in becoming more effective and productive. It relies on the time-proven practices explored in *The One Minute Manager* by Kenneth Blanchard and Spencer Johnson (William Morrow, 1982) and takes a refreshing look at them for today's world of instant everything, where you are expected to run before you have even been taught to walk.

It is my hope the up-to-date methods and practices included in this book encourage you to slow down so that you can go fast, to spend time on the basics. You'll not only keep up, you'll far surpass others.

Chapter 1

Setting the Stage:
Strategic Planning and
Organizational Goal-Setting

The principles outlined in *The One Minute Manager* more than 25 years ago are simple. Basically, give employees clear direction. Discuss the goals frequently and reset them when necessary. Tell direct reports how you think they are doing compared to the goals, including positive and constructive feedback. Separate the performance from the person. These basic approaches are still important. However, the pace of change, the volume and complexity of data available, and the quickly evolving competitive landscape create a very different context for success—everything around the simple approaches has changed, and thus the tools and management styles must change as well.

Organizations are not the hierarchies of the past where a direct report always had one manager. Teams are now often global or matrixes set up so that individuals report into several managers. Decisions get made following instant connections via e-mail and instant messaging where tone, inflection, and body language are not visible components of the communication. Misinterpretation is a common occurrence. Project teams can work on things 24/7 when they are based around the globe—someone is always awake—but cultures and behaviors can differ dramatically from region to region. The workforce has more generations participating in it than we have ever had before, and each generation has different values, attitudes, desires, and beliefs. Employees today might report to someone new to the company even after they have been there for several years because performance versus tenure is the standard of achievement.

Today, a leader or manager can spend minutes compiling data from an Internet search that might have taken months or even years 25 years ago. Progress can be made on a project or problem on one side of the globe while the other side of the globe sleeps. Walk into most companies today and you are likely to see a computer on every desk, people of all ages and races, and both genders working together side by side. Employees are almost as likely to report to someone younger than they are as they are to report to someone older. Tenure is down to less than two years for most job roles versus lifelong employment 25 years ago.

This book is designed to explore and present tools, tips, and practices that work for leaders and managers in today's context. Considering all that has changed around the simple approaches, it is important to consider what you can do to provide the type of leadership and support today's employee demands.

I first read *The One Minute Manager* in my late 20s (not quite 25 years ago!) while working in a large manufacturing facility. I was interested in developing myself and had several mentors both within and outside the company. They recommended it after attending a "leading edge" management class. I remember thinking how great it would be to have a manager actually practice the three principles. You would think that in manufacturing it is critical to have clear goals and measurables, but it was not the case then, and I have rarely seen it since.

Over the years, as my business book library, as well as management and leadership responsibilities, grew, I often referred back to *The One Minute Manager* to remind myself how simple it could be to do the right things as far as managing others. I never forgot how much I desired the clarity of goals and feedback as an employee. Even today, after more than 20 years in business, I find I need to constantly remind myself to make sure I cover the basics. There are a great deal of complicated choices available—more books with "the answer" and Internet searches providing thousands of options a mere click away. This book will help you perform the basics well in today's environments.

> *"Would you tell me please which way I ought to go from here?"*
>
> *"That depends a good deal on where you want to get to," said the Cat.*
>
> *"I don't much care where," said Alice.*
>
> *"Then it doesn't much matter which way you go," said the Cat.*
>
> —from *Alice's Adventure in Wonderland* by Lewis Carroll

The Evolution of Goal-Setting

Goal-setting is presented as the first of the *secrets* in *The One Minute Manager*. Today, goal-setting can really be viewed as one of the primary ways to set yourself, your team, and/or your organization up for success. Think about how you remember to do things or stay focused on certain tasks. Most of us use some sort of to-do list. It might be a structured list noted in your computer or you might just have reminders stuck around your work space. Visual cues help us stay on track.

Goal-setting and the broader process of strategic planning force you to pause and think, ponder options, and explore alternatives. It engages the brains and minds of others, and puts measures in front of you to keep you on track despite all the competing forces that vie for your time and attention. When done effectively, strategic planning and goal-setting dramatically increase your chances of achieving success.

Yet according to numerous studies, and especially when you ask employees, effective goal-setting is a rare practice in business today. I seldom work in organizations, whether large or small, mature or start-up, where employees can answer the questions:

- What are your top priorities?

- What are the three primary objectives you need to achieve this year/this quarter/this week?

- What will you be measured on at the end of the year?

- How will you know you have been successful after you have worked so hard this quarter/ month/week?

- How will you know if the company has been successful this year?

I have worked in organizations where leaders and managers swear to me that everyone can answer these questions easily. Although not usually fun to prove them wrong right up front (and sometimes not conducive to ongoing work), it is often necessary just to get the attention and resources required to implement a thorough goal-setting or strategic-planning process. It is a funny thing in organizations, because leaders know goal-setting and planning are the right things to do. They logically understand the value of it and the need to be clear with all employees on what is important to focus on. So why do we rarely see it being done?

There are probably a hundred answers to this question. Twenty-five years ago, the world moved at a very different pace. Just watch a television show or movie from the early 1980s and you will be quickly reminded of a time when our pace was slower. Perhaps the pace of activity around us today stops us from taking the time up front to clarify, quantify, and determine *what* and *how* we will measure progress at work. Or perhaps it is that goal-setting can sometimes be incredibly tedious. It may even be that most leaders have thought about where they want things to go for so long that they just cannot imagine the employees are not all thinking the same things. No matter the barriers or reasons we do not do goal-setting more often, it can be a simple and yet significant set of activities that create value for the entire organization.

The bottom line is: Figure out what is getting in your way and work to remove the beliefs, the thoughts, the rationalizations that stop you from spending time and energy on strategic planning and goal-setting. As the leader of a company, a team, a division, or just yourself, you can make a difference in achieving desired results more effectively. The framework, tips, and guidance that follow do not have to be complicated, lengthy, or difficult. Go through the materials and choose what works for you. With small teams, you can get through the initial process in an afternoon. If you are doing strategic planning for an organization, plan on spending several full days over a series of weeks or months. If you are doing goal-setting for yourself, set aside a few hours to note what you think you should focus on, and then an hour to discuss and review it with your manager. Do this periodically because change is certain to occur.

In *The One Minute Manager*, goal-setting is defined as clarifying what an individual's responsibilities are and what that person is being held accountable for. This basic premise is still important, but there are more moving parts, going faster, and typically a broader context within which you must set

goals today. Twenty-five years ago, a thorough or more ho-
listic approach was not typically used. The simple command-
and-control style fit those hierarchical, slower-paced
environments.

When I work with leaders who are absolutely certain everyone knows the goals and is clear on the end state, I
often ask them to get an image in their minds of themselves as track stars. They have just broken through the
tape at the end of a race. Then I ask them to get an
image in their minds of where the rest of the organization is. Are they even at the stadium yet? Have they
stretched? Are they really in the race? Are they running
just behind you or are they at the starting blocks? Are
some folks ahead and on to the next race? Are others in a
different stadium or even playing a different sport?

When someone has a tough time slowing down
enough for others to catch up, this image can be printed
and posted in front of him or her each morning as a
reminder. Visual cues help us stay focused and they serve
as good reminders. As a leader, your job is to figure out
which event at the track to compete in, which races to
run, how to get the skills needed on the team to win, and
how to keep all the athletes operating in optimum condi-
tion. A thorough strategic-planning and goal-setting process will help you accomplish all of this.

Today, I typically find that leaders and managers assume
there is clarity in the organization, or, if they do realize it is
not company-wide, they feel strongly there is certainly clarity
within their own team or division. Common refrains include:
"But of course employees are aligned. Of course employees
know what they need to focus on. Everyone here knows what

they have to do it and they just get it done. We don't need to do formal goal-setting...." "We talk about goals once a year, so everyone knows what to do." I have even been told that "goal-setting is just that mamsy pamsy human resources stuff. That is not what we need to focus on in this company." Never mind that in that company, employees were confused, working on completely different agendas, and generally ineffective. In fact, individuals were working long hours and putting in a lot of effort on competing agendas. The senior leaders of the company could not understand why so little got done and why it took so long to get anything done at all. The employees could not understand why they were constantly asked to do things other than what they thought they should be working on. All in all, everyone was working hard, but working on a lot of different agendas (and, by the way, they were losing market share, had declining profitability, and lacked product innovation). This is a perfect example of working hard and not working smart, which is a topic I will address throughout the book.

Working with companies on goal-setting and a broader strategic-planning process can be a real adventure in exploration and inspiration. It can also be just like a day at the zoo. Look at that animal there with his head in the ground, or that one over there, boasting the big colorful feathers but flying nowhere, or that one there, making a lot of noise all about nothing. And how about the ones doing the same things over and over but getting no real results? Entertaining for those of us on the outside of the fence, but not a style to mimic if you are working to become a high-performing organization.

When we embark on goal-setting or strategic planning at any level in an organization, we have to be committed to invest the time and energy required to do it well, communicate it broadly, and hold ourselves and others accountable to deliver. Consistency and clarity of goals across the organization are required to maintain focus and alignment in today's fast-moving and intensely competitive environments. Leaders must be able to constantly scan the environment, take in data from a multitude of sources, assess and determine the impact on the company, and communicate adjustments quickly. Managers must be able to serve as the primary interface between their direct reports and the overall organization, translating top-line strategies into achievable projects or initiatives. They must be able to note deviations from the course in a timely manner and act to realign resources quickly.

There are numerous layers within most organizations, and there are goal-setting and strategic-planning elements that are appropriate at each layer. First let me define what we will use in this book as the definitions of strategic planning and goal-setting. Strategic planning includes the entire process: determining why you exist, where you are headed, how you will behave to get there, and what value you have to stakeholders. It includes short-term specifics including individual and team goals for a one-year time frame. I recommend three-year time frames for longer-term direction to most of my clients considering how much and how quickly the world changes today. Strategies are general categories or themes that help all stakeholders understand what will take up most of the attention and resources.

> Think of your employees as water. Provide a container and direct the flow, and you will create extraordinary power. Carving out streambeds and moving mountains is easy work. But take the same amount of water and scatter it like raindrops over a large area and you'll achieve virtually no effect.
>
> Just imagine the Grand Canyon as you consider how powerful focus and alignment can be for any organization.

Goal-setting is a subset of strategic planning. The time frame is generally one year and it is more bound by measures. Goal-setting notes tactics or actions that must occur and when they must occur. It is more specific than strategic planning but must support the strategies outlined for the organization. Goal-setting as defined in *The One Minute Manager* does not necessarily consider this broader context. Goal-setting today must be more strongly linked to the big picture to be effective. Today's employees crave an understanding of the *why* coupled with the *what*.

Organizational Goal-Setting
The strategic planning framework

A thorough strategic-planning process for an organization has the following components:

- ❧ A Mission (why the organization exists).

- ❧ Guiding Principles or Organizational Attributes (how you expect people to behave).

> ● Value Propositions (the value you have to each of your stakeholder groups, both internal and external).

> ● Vision Statements (in this book they are called Destination Points to minimize the ongoing chatter about the definition of mission versus vision) (where the organization will get to within a specified time frame).

> ● Strategies or areas of focus (how the organization will get there in a broad sense).

A comprehensive process also requires action planning or breakthrough modeling to note what it will really take to get to where you want to go. You have to put the plan into action and operationalize it. During that process you will determine the Organizational Capabilities necessary (the required systems, processes, tools, and technology that need to be in place to achieve the strategies).

Defining team and individual accountabilities is also critical. This links the big picture to individual goals and competencies. Like any puzzle, all the pieces need to be in place to achieve the desired effect.

Clearly defined and articulated goals and milestones are critical to the long-term success of the enterprise. Employees want and need to know the bigger picture. The mission and strategies can serve to inspire and energize employees, and create pride and connection throughout the organization. They act as a sort of beacon that supports keeping all activities and efforts aligned.

The process of *organizational strategic planning* is also critical. When all employees are involved in determining the components of the organizational goals, there is generally deeper understanding of what they mean as well as greater buy-in and alignment for achieving them. However, due to time, financial, and other resource constraints, this is not always possible.

Approach	Overview	Advantages	Disadvantages
Proclaiming	Most components of the organizational goal-setting are established by a small group of company leaders or even a singular individual. "This is what we are doing. Get excited and get on board."	➤ Can be done with clarity. ➤ Appropriate in a crisis or urgent situation where there is no time to engage others in the process initially.	➤ Somewhat authoritarian approach that can backfire. ➤ Does not allow for input, collaboration, or discussion, which can stifle innovation and engagement with the mission, strategies, and goals.
Persuading	Most components of the organizational goal-setting are established by a small group of company leaders. "This is how we will succeed. Isn't this great?"	➤ If employees believe it is good for them, they will typically sign on. ➤ If there is trust in place, employees want to believe the organization will be successful, so they will engage.	➤ Achieving compliance is easy, getting commitment is not and may be hard to discern. ➤ Going overboard on the "sales speak" may come off as insincere and shallow.
Testing	Components of the organizational goal-setting are established in draft form and then leadership seeks input. "Look what we have come up with. What do you think?"	➤ Those closest to your customer can express themselves. ➤ An initial draft provides some focus for the feedback. ➤ If I have input, I feel valued and am more likely to buy into it later.	➤ The approach can take a lot of time depending on how much input and how many employees participate. ➤ If input is not incorporated into the final version, employees may be angry and resentful.
Collaborating	A framework and process is put in place, and input is sought, compiled, and distilled from all levels of the organization. "This is where we believe we should go. We are in this together."	➤ The framework and process provide structure. ➤ Employees like to share their opinions and input and usually feel more valued when they can do so. ➤ If employees create it, they get it and often try harder to live it.	➤ This approach is lengthy and requires numerous resources, including time, facilitation, and analysis. ➤ Ongoing input is hard to manage and incorporate.

There is a variety of approaches for setting organizational goals. Each approach, like most things in life, has its advantages and disadvantages. There is no perfect way. Typically, some combination of these approaches summarized in the chart shown on page 25 will work best for you.

Think through the advantages and disadvantages of each approach as well as your current state. Remain realistic when you determine which path to take. It is worse to set out and announce to everyone that you are going to conduct a collaborative process and then turn around and take a more proclaiming approach. Whichever path you choose, just shoot straight with employees. It is better to say "we feel we can get through this more quickly if we use a small group to work on it" or "with everyone's plates so full these days, we think it is best if most people stay focused on their day-to-day responsibilities while a small team spends time on this...." When you don't tell employees the basics of what the decision is and why, the stories employees will make up to fill the void of information is going to be much worse than the truth. I often find myself in situations with senior-level employees trying to shed light on what leadership thought was a simple decision or having conversations about "just what is going on around here?" when really nothing very exciting is happening. I continue to be amazed at our capacity and tendency to create very innovative reasons or attribute negative intentions to what are usually simple situations. So just tell it like it is.

A few decades ago a proclaiming approach was typical and actually expected. Employees were much more likely to be told what to do with little input. Today's workforce requires more. Employees want to understand the *why* and desire the ability to have input. Even if you choose a proclaiming approach today, understand the disadvantages and include actions to mitigate the risks with this style.

Consider the following in determining which methodology you will use:

Your current business conditions

➤ Is there a need to change quickly? (You are near bankruptcy, an investor pulled out, a new competitive product made yours obsolete, board pressure, etc.)

➤ Has your market suddenly shifted dramatically? (There are new regulations, breakthrough products, and so on.)

➤ Are there competitors that have recently had a significant affect on your success and/or future?

Your leadership credibility and trust levels

➤ Is there trust in the organization?

➤ Are employees generally engaged?

➤ Have you recently experienced a disruptive event such as a merger or acquisition that caused some confusion?

Resource availability

➤ How much time and money do you have to invest in the process?

➤ Can you afford not to invest in the process?

➤ What will you give up and what will you get?

Your leadership and management style

➤ Do you really want input or are you so clear that you don't have the tolerance for others' ideas?

➤ What is your most comfortable style? If you are a natural salesperson, it will be difficult to sincerely lead a process without using those skills.

➤ What skills do you need to develop to do an effective job with your chosen approach and how will you get them?

➤ How often and from whom will you get feedback on how well the entire process is going?

Really think about these questions and try to be brutally honest with yourself in answering them. If you have a trusted source from inside or outside who will give you direct, candid feedback in some of these areas, get it! This is not the time to step gingerly. Determining how you go about strategic planning has far-reaching implications for you and the organization. You don't want to spend months and months to find out you discounted the credibility, motivation, and engagement in the company so significantly that, no matter what you say, no one is listening or following. Alternatively, you don't want to proceed with a comprehensive, fully inclusive strategy if you can leverage the trust in the organization, involve a smaller team, and move more quickly. Employees today are not likely to follow blindly. Leaders come and go all too often, the competitive landscape can change in the blink of an eye, and employees' options are greater than ever before.

Unfortunately, determining the approach to strategic planning is often completely discounted in planning efforts. Sometimes the executive team is on a one-year turnover plan (none of them ever make it longer than one year at the company) and employees believe that, no matter what you say or do, they will outlast you. This makes it easy to keep working on individual agendas or favorite projects, so employees ignore any direction on goals that are contrary to what they believe is important or interesting or glamorous. Sometimes a leader is passionate about strategies and goals but lacks credibility in implementation, so it is easy for employees to nod emphatically in the meeting and laugh later in the breakroom about what will really occur. Often there is great intention on the part of the planning team but plain old misunderstanding, confusion, or negative assumptions by others about what is going on and how it will impact each individual. These negatives most often prevail.

How many great stories have you heard at the office when leaders and managers are holed up in meetings for days on end? I have heard a lot over the years. I am always impressed by the imagination but confounded on the origins of such stories as "they are not involving us because we are all going to be laid off when our competitor acquires us," or "they don't care what we think or know; they believe they know it all," or "I know the CEO and all she cares about is..." or "no matter what gets written down, what always gets done is only what (insert name of loud and squeaky senior leader here) wants." Let's hope you were never one of the creative geniuses covering up your own uncertainty by devising these stories, but you probably have heard a few over the years.

Legitimately, there is more cynicism in the workplaces of today. After all, we have seen *Fortune* 500s vanish as a result of unethical and illegal practices. We have watched political figures globally get caught in scandal after scandal, and even some of our religious leaders have fallen quite short of what we all hoped for. Over the course of several decades, employee trust has severely eroded. Keep all of this in mind so that you create a much higher chance of success in your organization.

Once you have determined the approach that is right for your team and/or the organization, review the framework shown on page 30 and use it as a structure to map out the organizational goals. Renaming pieces and parts of it are fine as long as the definitions are clear to everyone in the organization. Try not to get caught in the trap of the never ending discussion about what is a mission versus a vision. (That is a whole different book!) Just choose labels that work in your environment and define them in a way that works in your organization.

Organizational Goal-Setting
The strategic planning framework

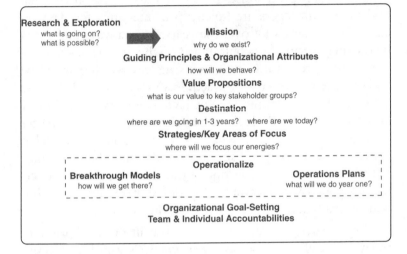

Research & Exploration
what is going on?
what is possible?

Mission
why do we exist?

Guiding Principles & Organizational Attributes
how will we behave?

Value Propositions
what is our value to key stakeholder groups?

Destination
where are we going in 1-3 years?   where are we today?

Strategies/Key Areas of Focus
where will we focus our energies?

Operationalize

Breakthrough Models
how will we get there?

Operations Plans
what will we do year one?

Organizational Goal-Setting
Team & Individual Accountabilities

Get Clear: Know What You Know and What You Don't Know

Most leaders and managers feel confident that they understand the industry, competitors, and partners fairly well. However, I find it incredibly helpful to force organizations to go through a short research and exploration phase before doing any goal-setting or strategic planning. You will be amazed at what the data and facts can tell you that are different from the currently held beliefs (even your own). I often work with clients to uncover the areas to explore and then assign an "expert" (someone on the planning team who may or may not really have expertise in the area assigned), who is responsible for researching and presenting a summary to the team. Sometimes assigning someone unfamiliar with a topic or area is most effective, as that individual has fewer limiting beliefs about *what is today* and *what is possible*. These presentations are intended to inform, educate, and inspire. They should be data-based presentations leading the team to better understand *what is* and think about *what is possible*.

Industries and companies used to be fairly stable. Today, entire sectors are created in a matter of weeks and others fade away as quickly as they arose. New products and services are introduced at a pace that is tough to digest. Spend the time to get the facts on what is currently going on in and around your business. You might be surprised at what has changed since you last took a look.

There are numerous tools that are readily available to assist you in this phase. The Internet is probably the fastest and most cost effective. Use a variety of search engines and search criteria to explore. In addition, look internally. A plethora of useful data often exists buried in organizations. Check for surveys and studies. Recently I worked with a company and while in the lunchroom overheard a group from marketing talking about the $100K they had just spent on some marketing studies. They were chatting about how surprised they were regarding some of the findings. I eavesdropped for as long as I could and then made darn sure we used that data in the planning sessions. The senior executives were not really aware it existed even though they had approved the expenditure!

Talk to frontline employees particularly if you have a customer-service function. Ask them to tell you the top three things they would change to make customers more satisfied/ spend more/buy more. Check professional associations that serve your industry or serve the same customers you target. They are also a wonderful source of information.

➤ Typical areas covered in the research phase include:

  ❧ Competitors.

- Latest technologies in the sector/beside the sector.

- Partners/alliances.

- Regions (geographic or demographic oriented).

- Customers/consumers (history and trends).

- Complimentary services and products.

- Similar and dissimilar business models (franchises, global, subscription, and services).

- Complementary sectors—what influences your product or service (how is it used and when).

- Adjacent sectors (what is purchased before or after your product/service, what could it be combined with?).

I also encourage leaders to look at business models, groups, or companies that are completely different than their own but that do something particularly well. For instance, in working with a not-for-profit arts organization, I encouraged them to research the Association for the Advancement of Retired Persons (AARP). It is one of the largest and most successful member organizations in the world. I was fairly certain there could be some good learning by looking at AARP and considering what could be duplicated, borrowed, and done similarly. The research was of tremendous value and significantly influenced the strategies of the group, even though the products of the researched organization varied greatly from the one doing the planning.

As a general guideline, structure each "expert" presentation in the following way:

➤ Note the general approach you took.

- Where did you look?

- Who did you talk to?
- What reports did you find?
➤ Note the data you found by key point/finding.
  - Facts, figures, and types (for example, products, revenue expected within what time frames, industry leaders in the area, technology, and customer insights).
➤ Note any recommendations you have or points you think should be considered in this area.
  - What got you excited as you researched this area?
➤ What do you believe is possible based on what you found?
  - What should definitely be considered?
  - What should the team consider considering?
  - What does not seem to fit with who the company is?
➤ Also note any outstanding questions or comments you have in this topic area.

Keep an open mind when researching and presenting. Try to prove yourself wrong a few times, especially if you have strongly held opinions about something. Really work to open yourself to possibilities by asking, "What if...

- I am wrong?"
- there is something else?"
- it could be interpreted another way?"
- there is more I know/do not know about this?"

There are three key reasons we do not use "what if" thinking more often. Firstly, when we look at new ideas, we tend to be critical and focus on the negative. Secondly, it is fairly unlikely that just one "what if" question will produce a practical answer. You may have to ask many. Thirdly, we don't use tools we have not been taught. We *are* taught to focus on what we consider reality, and that severely limits "'what if' thinking.

You may want to do a SWOT (Strengths, Weaknesses, Opportunities, Threats) analysis at this point in your process to assist in determining areas of research and exploration. The understanding you gain from this analysis can be valuable and will assist you in the definition of your end state. A SWOT analysis helps you uncover your internal strengths and weaknesses as well as the opportunities and threats in your external environment.

SWOTs are:	
Strengths:	What do we excel at? What is difficult for others to copy?
Weaknesses:	Where do we have risks or limitations that get in our way?
Opportunities:	What exists that we can capitalize on or leverage?
Threats:	What are we concerned about in the external environment? What are our competitors likely to do? Are we at risk for additional competitors?

Correct identification of SWOTs is essential because subsequent steps in the process of planning are based in part on addressing the SWOTs.

Points to ponder as you consider significant Strengths:

● Where have we really been able to excel?

● Is there something we have that we don't use/do enough?

- Is there something we can develop quickly that we can leverage?

- What do others say is our greatest strength?

Points to ponder as you consider Weaknesses:

- What has gotten in our way in the past?

- How do we get in our own way?

- What processes do we have for identifying weaknesses in the organization, and how well do these processes work?

  - ▶ What processes do we have for remediating the deficiencies identified, and how well do they work?

- What functional silos are scattered across the organization? What groups work on their own with little to no interaction with others?

- Are you monitoring signs and signals from the marketplace that can both support your expectations, if appropriate, and provide strong evidence when new paths are desirable or necessary?

Points to ponder as you consider Opportunities:

- Is there a product, a customer relationship, or a market presence that we can better leverage?

- Is there something we would pursue if we had more resources (such as people, dollars, or time)?

- What is our competitor most worried we will do? Should we?

- What signals are key to assessing our relationships with our market/customers?

- How diverse is our portfolio of business relationships and opportunities? Are there numerous ways to succeed?

❧ What investments are we making whose primary returns will be in the long term?

❧ Are our plans formulated in ways that they will support adapting to evolving or new market opportunities, including unexpected opportunities?

Points to ponder as you consider Threats:

❧ What are we most concerned about?

❧ Are new/different competitors likely to emerge?

❧ Is there a potential supply problem?

❧ Do we have good relationships with employees, vendors, and customers?

General questions to consider now and as you progress through the process:

❧ What proportions of our organization's resources are focused on maintaining and enhancing the status quo?

❧ How much time do we spend leading and nurturing new directions?

❧ What new efforts have we started in the past year? What efforts have we stopped?

❧ Is our long-term thinking focused on the few critical things that matter? Are we vigilantly avoiding the many possible diversions?

❧ Do we have the people and financial resources to execute our plans successfully?

❧ Do near-term problems and opportunities frequently preempt long-term plans and undermine progress?

❧ Does it seem like the rest will be easy once we have finished our plans?

Once you have determined the SWOTs, think through the following in preparing to draft destination points:

1. How can we use each Strength?
2. How can we stop or mitigate each Weakness?
3. How can we exploit each Opportunity?
4. How can we defend against each Threat?

Internal factors / External factors	Strengths (S) List 5 to 10 internal strengths	Weaknesses (W) List 5 to 10 internal weaknesses
Opportunities (O) List 5 to 10 external opportunities	Generate ideas and strategies that use your strengths to take advantage of the opportunities	Generate ideas and strategies that take advantage of your opportunities in the market by overcoming weaknesses
Threats (T) List 5 to 10 external threats	Generate ideas and strategies that use your strengths to avoid pending or potential threats	Generate ideas and strategies that help you avoid threats and overcome your weaknesses

This process lends itself to brainstorming to create alternative strategies for your breakthrough model (see **Creating a Breakthrough Model** on page 54). It forces leaders and managers to create growth and retrenchment approaches. It also assists you in gaining clarity on strengths and weaknesses internally as well as both real and imagined external opportunities and threats.

Presenting data-based information is a powerful way to begin strategic planning or goal-setting. So much of the time we walk around with mental models of *what is* that are quite different than *what actually is*. I have watched leaders argue vehemently for something prior to data being presented that clearly negated the point. I have seen managers work hard for long periods of time knowing absolutely, positively that something is so, only to find it is not so. This often happens in the areas of customer insights. If we work in development, we just know that adding that next product feature will make all the difference. If we work in marketing, we know that if we could just spend more to reach more people, they would surely buy. If we work in finance, we are certain that we can become more cost efficient even if we are underinvesting. And so it goes.

> **Key Operating Practice:** Get real while doing a SWOT analysis. Involve those closest to the areas you are examining. Make sure each voice is heard and as many perspectives as possible are explored.

Twenty-five years ago, our SWOT analysis was much simpler. After all, barriers to entry in most sectors were higher—there was no Internet to equalize some of the largest marketing departments with one creative individual working from his garage. Today you must consider more. Because everything is changing so rapidly, just when you think you have explored enough, it all changes again.

Each of us walks around with a limited approximation of reality in our minds at all times. Sometimes the more we know about something, the less we really know because we are constantly viewing the world through our filters. The research and exploration phase helps us to expand the lens with which we view the world. It is intended to open our minds to *what is* and help us think more broadly about *what could be*.

Know Why: Define Your Reason for Being
Mission

A compelling mission statement tells others why *you* exist, described in the present tense, as if it were happening now. After you have come up with a few thoughts on your mission statement, consider the following:

- Aspirational: Is it big, compelling, and broad reaching?

- Brevity: Is it brief and to the point?

- Clarity: Is it easy to understand?

- Specific: Does it reflect your unique characteristics (your passion, what you can be the best at)?

- General: Is it broad enough to include evolving business needs?

- Pride: Are you glad to be a part of it?

- Inspiration: Does it compel you to work toward realizing it?

There are many great mission statements that have been developed for organizations. If one does not come to you quickly, do a search and look at the statements for other organizations you admire, your competitors, high-performing organizations, and so on. Alternatively, have all the participants in the process jot down the key phrases or words that come immediately to mind when they consider why you exist. Have each participant share his or her notes, discuss the input, and then assign a small team of two or three to wordsmith the phrases or words into something that meets all the criteria of a compelling mission statement.

Make sure your mission statement answers the question of *why* you exist versus where you are going or what you might do.

Some sample mission statements:

> **Key Operating Practice**: Never try to have a group of more than three people wordsmith a mission statement. Gather input and thoughts from as many others as you want involved in the process, and then create a small team to manipulate the words. Writing by a large committee is a painful and usually inefficient practice.

- ❧ We are a company focused on solving some of the world's toughest problems.

- ❧ We are the leading global provider of travel experiences by inspiring travelers everywhere.

- ❧ We exist to benefit and refresh everyone it (our product) touches.

- ❧ To bring inspiration and innovation to every athlete* in the world. *if you have a body, you are an athlete.

- ❧ Organizing the world's information and making it universally accessible and useful.

- ❧ Our business is discovering, developing and delivering novel medicines and vaccines that can make a difference in people's lives.

◉ We provide relief to victims of disasters and help people prevent, prepare for, and respond to emergencies.

◉ We are ladies and gentlemen serving ladies and gentlemen.

◉ Providing physicians with comprehensive solutions to treat chronic diseases and individualize patient care.

◉ We help businesses and people throughout the world realize their full potential.

The more richly detailed and visual the image is, the more compelling your mission will be. Your mission is the longest lasting piece of your strategic framework or plan. It should not change frequently. Reread the mission statements here. They are big. They are bold. They are compelling. They encompass myriad possibilities for the organization and are not usually tied to specific products or services. They withstand the test of time. Yours should too.

Act Right: Describe How to Behave

Guiding principles and organizational attributes

Your principles and attributes describe how you will behave with each other as well as with other stakeholders. They note what you will do when faced with difficult situations or challenges. They are excellent benchmarks to refer back to and measure against on a continuous basis to ensure you are achieving your goals in a way that you believe is best. They are also always written in the present tense, as if you are already behaving according to the definitions. You might decide to use values instead of principles or attributes. They are similar in that they describe how you expect people to behave. I chose to use guiding principles or organizational attributes with most of my clients so there are not lengthy discussions and heated conversations about what is a value versus something else. I find it is just easier to call them something that does not have as much emotional connotation associated with it as "values" does. Use whatever works best for you.

When you are defining your guiding principles and organizational attributes, consider the following:

> Real: Is it achievable and realistic?

> Hierarchy: Do you need to establish a hierarchy so that, when conflict occurs, you can be clear on what behavior is most important?

> Guiding: Does it create clear guidance on what to do and how to behave?

> Measurable: Can you define it so that it can be measured and continuously improved?

> Pride: Is it an attribute you are proud of?

Sample operating principles and organizational attributes:

❧ We are performance-driven and strive for continuous improvement.

❧ We do what is right and operate with the highest levels of integrity.

❧ We are team-oriented.

❧ We are client-focused.

❧ We are innovative.

❧ We are trustworthy.

❧ We are passionate about what we do.

❧ We treat the business as if it were our own.

❧ We move quickly and with discipline.

❧ We are transparent—open and honest in all that we do.

- We treat each other with respect and courtesy.

- We have a diverse workplace and respect differences in opinions and work styles.

- We listen to our customers and respond with sincerity, honesty, and courtesy.

- We set reasonable but high expectations and then work to exceed them.

- We are constantly looking at the future and discussing "what's possible?" and "what's next?"

- We are devoted to building the best company possible.

- We are clear on our common goals and work together to reach them.

- We have clear accountability and line of sight throughout the organization.

- We are a learning organization.

- We develop and use continuous feedback loops between stakeholders and across functions.

- We utilize world-class quality-control processes.

- We are an employer of choice.

> **Key Operating Practice:** Of course, these all sound great, but try to force yourself to come up with five to seven that you will truly adhere to. When the going gets tough and you have to make cuts or difficult decisions, which ones will you hold as sacred? Which ones are you willing to invest in?

Sample values include:

❧ Integrity.

❧ Trustworthy.

❧ Innovative.

❧ Customer-focused.

> **Key Operating Practice:** Define your guiding principles or values with behavioral examples (what does it look like if it is being done well in your organization?). I also recommend defining contraindicators (what is out of bounds or what does it not look like so there are clear guide rails for each desired behavior or value?).

Another way to determine behaviors that are important to the organization and/or team, or as a complement to your operating principles is to think through various attributes and values that might be used to describe and/or define any organization. Consider the words you prefer used by customers/clients, employees, or other stakeholders to describe your organization. Encourage those providing input to think about your organization or team as if it were behaving/doing things the way they want them done. Ask them to focus on desired state versus current state.

Get input from as many people as possible, including customers, shareholders, and even competitors, when you can. I often find that this input is quite surprising to leaders of an organization. Sometimes strong perceptions about who you are or who/what people want you to be are different from your own. In addition, using a data-based approach to getting clarity on your values and/or operating practices can help you understand the gap between where you are and where you want to be. This insight can then be incorporated in your goal-setting so that you are constantly moving toward your desired state.

I recently worked with one organization that talked about customer focus a great deal. We conducted a short internal survey on how each employee defined customer focus and what he or she did to demonstrate it on a daily basis. We then compared that to data on what customers wanted. Not only did definitions and actions of employees vary dramatically, but they were not aligned with what customers really wanted. Individuals were certain they were living the value, but customers did not see it that way. We ended up changing the value from customer focus to customer obsessive and defined it clearly including behavioral examples.

> **Key Operating Practice:** When you seek input from others, be sure to let them know what you heard and what you are going to do with the input. Be careful not to over-promise that you will do or become what each stakeholder wants. Also acknowledge the value of hearing from multiple perspectives.

I often coach clients to describe for me what the value or behavior looks like if it is being done well. What do I see, hear, think, and feel when I interact with you? If you can describe your guiding principles or values in this manner, it will be easier to get employees aligned.

The following is a list you can use as a survey to seek input from others to inform your decisions. Add other words that have meaning to you and your organization/team.

Visionary
Considers Profitability
Makes a Difference
Streamlined
Forceful
Supportive
Leaders
Thoughtful
Empowered
Safe Source
Business Partner
Decentralized
Cooperative
Open
Committed
Warm
Powerful
Loyal
Customer-Focused
Innovative
Fast
Passionate
Task-Driven
Specialists
Team-Oriented
Accurate
Enlightened
Caring
Creative
Best Anywhere

Performing
Engaging
Enthusiastic
Controlled
People-Oriented
Cohesive
Proud
Serious
Excellent
Fun
Achieving
Driven
Entrepreneurial
Cutting Edge
Insightful
Conservative
Participative
Rewards Talent
Determined
Flexible
Experts
Reliable
Future-Oriented
Capable
Focused
Knowledgeable
Harmonious
Decisive
Honest

Where To? Identify Your Desired End State
Destination points/vision

> *"Physiologically impossible or not, I just saw myself doing it."*
>
> —Roger Bannister, first man to break the four-minute mile

Your destination statements, sometimes called your vision, describe where you are going. The more clarity you can create on what it looks like at the end state, the more likely you are to get there. Everyone told Roger Bannister that it was impossible to run a four-minute mile. His response is noted above. The week after he broke the world record, someone else did as well, and many others followed. It was not impossible to run a four-minute mile; someone just had to get very clear and envision success to get there. Many Olympic athletes use an approach known as "success visioning" to achieve their goals. Imagine winning—being the best at what you do as an organization—and now describe it in as much detail as possible. What will I hear when I am there? What will

Key Operating Practice:
Similar to a travel brochure or Website that tells you what you can expect when you arrive, a destination statement must be very clear. It has to be exciting and inspirational as well as believable and achievable. Gather input from as many as are involved in your process and then create small sub-teams to finalize each destination point.

I see? What will I be doing? If you can picture getting there, your chances of doing it increase dramatically.

Your destination statements are intended to generate visions in the minds of each and every employee. These images can be powerful motivators and guide rails to keep everyone moving forward in the right direction. Because we often use the same words to mean very different things, destination points are critical to gain shared understanding. I worked in one company that constantly said it was "best in class." When employees were surveyed, more than 50 percent said they had no idea what that meant or how to work towards it, and the other 50 percent had incredibly diverse views on it. It looked good on the break-room wall, but really meant nothing.

In today's fast-paced times, destination statements generally encompass a three-year time frame. Beyond that, you are likely just guessing as to what is possible. The statements note what it looks like when you arrive at your destination. A destination statement paints a vivid picture for everyone and generates ongoing motivation to get there. It provides cohesion, direction, and behavioral guidance. It tells everyone what you are doing, what you are not doing, and what you will be doing when you get to where you want to go. It does not have to be just one statement. Consider creating destination statements for each critical area of your organization. I often use the categories and worksheet shown on page 49 as a starting point with my clients.

Once you have completed them, check it against the following criteria:

- ❧ Consistency: Is it consistent with the mission statement?

- ❧ Clarity: Is it easy to understand? Is it easy to tell what is in and what is out? Does it tell you what you need to do (directionally)?

- ❧ Specific: Does it provide enough details to initiate a level of measurement? Does it paint a picture I can relate to and a place I can envision?

Categories	What it looks like when we get there...
Key operating achievements (the big three or four)?	
How the workplace culture will be, including the attitudes, beliefs, values, and operating principles?	
What skills/knowledge/abilities will exist? ► Business Unit or Division Level ► Company-wide	
What organizational structures will be in place? ► Business Unit or Division Level ► Company-wide	
What work processes and metrics will be used?	
What tools, systems, and technology are necessary? ► Internal vs. External	
What products will be in market? What products will be in development?	
Who will our customers be? How many will we have?	
Who will our competitors be/what types of companies will we compete against? Greatest competitive advantage/threat?	
How will we be known?	
What will our brand represent?	

- ❧ Flexible: Is it flexible enough to include evolving business needs?

- ❧ Pride: Are you glad to be a part of the effort?

- ❧ Inspiration: Does it compel you to want to go there?

Maintaining commitment and action is challenging in any organization. It is common for organizations and managers to lack follow-up processes, to lose focus on the long-term goals, and to be driven by non-productive daily activities. In addition, the past is often comfortable and compelling for employees because people think they understand what happened and why. It is important to make sure that the future is more compelling than the past. Your destination statement(s) should support addressing these challenges.

When *The One Minute Manager* was written more than 25 years ago, it was typical to create 10-year vision statements. Can you imagine trying to do that today? Pause for a moment and consider how much has happened/developed/changed in just the past 10 years, and how little of it any of us could have imagined 10 years ago. Dream big things **and** get clear on a shorter time frame to make it real.

I am often amazed and energized by the passion frontline employees have about what is possible in an organization. If you can engage them in the process, you will find they are a significant force in providing great descriptors for defining your destination points. Besides that, if you use the language of frontline employees right up front, you won't have to translate from business bingo/executive speak later!

Once you have clarity on your destination points, use the same categories and define current state. This will give you the information you need on what gaps must be addressed so that you can plan out appropriate action steps and time frames.

Who Cares? Note Your Value to Those Who Matter

Value propositions

> WIIFM
> (What's in it for me?)
>   Everyone's favorite radio station.

Your value propositions define the significance you have to your external stakeholders, such as customers and suppliers. They answer the question "what's in it for me?" It is the one phrase you want a customer to say about you if asked why he/she purchases your services/products. A value proposition is a helpful statement if you have recently changed the focus of your organization or completed a merger or acquisition that shifts the value you have externally. It is also helpful if a new group is formed within a company and you are initiating goal-setting for that group. The statement can help make it clear why the group/division was formed, what differentiates the group/division from others, and what value it has externally.

> **Key Operating Practice:** If you are defining your value to customers, ask customers what they think. Get source data whenever possible.

This is always an area of great discussion in strategic planning sessions I have facilitated. The common belief going in is that this will be simple. After all, isn't it clear what value we have? You will be amazed at the variance in truths about what you offer to customers, employees, and partners. Open and candid conversations about your desired value is important as it exposes differing thoughts and opinions, and, when done well, offers you a wonderful opportunity to increase value to your stakeholders through incorporating a broader range of perspectives.

When considering who the stakeholders are, make sure to consider upper management if you are a team or division. Sometimes overlooked, this can be a powerful stakeholder who you want to keep satisfied!

Sample introductory verbiage for a value proposition:

- As an indispensable business partner, we provide superior....

- As a trusted source, we provide the best experience and expertise to....

- As the leader of innovation in X, we establish the standards and....

- As an employer, we offer a learning environment....

This is yet another area that has changed dramatically in the past 25 years. Companies today often have a more diverse customer base, more diverse employees, more products or services, and almost assuredly more laws, regulations, and practices to adhere to. The discussions, engagement, and insight you can obtain from these sources are a valuable tool in gaining clarity and buy-in throughout the organization.

Get Simple: Determine Areas of Focus

Strategies

Once you achieve clarity on your destination points and value propositions, three to five core areas of focus are generally obvious. Keep the value propositions in front of you throughout the rest of the process so you can constantly consider whether or not your plans continue to deliver value to your stakeholders. Consider what must occur for you to reach your destination, including what economic engine(s) fuel your company.

The strategies are the areas of focus for the organization or the team. They are typically themes that cut across several destination points or areas of the company. Strategies help you leverage the 80-20 rule, the law of the vital few where 80 percent of the effect comes from 20 percent of the causes, to keep everyone focused. Actions to directly support these strategies are where you should see the most energy and focus in organizations. Narrowing to three to five strategies greatly assists in achieving alignment throughout the organization. Employees should be able to tell you what the core strategies are in the company at any given time. Strategies might be things such as:

- Build a platform for more effective delivery of products.

- Create a world-class strategic account management organization.

- Gain significant operating efficiencies.

- Deliver useful, timely, and consistent communication.

- Lead the market through innovation.

- Optimize internally by coordinating across functions.

- Migrate from products only to services and products.

- Expand our business model to include franchising.

- Become an employer of choice.

I find it particularly interesting when I do informal questioning of employees within the organizations where I consult.

Employees will sometimes share with you energetically how what they are working on directly supports a specific strategy. The only problem is, the strategy they are supporting was the one from two years ago! Strategies change and employees have to be kept up to date on current ones. Many employees work on long-term projects and easily lose sight of the bigger picture in the face of daily deadlines and other pressures. (See Chapter 2 for further ideas and guidance on communications.)

Make It Real: Operationalize Your Plan

Operationalizing your strategic plan

Now that you have the top part of your model complete, it is time to dive into the tedious but critical portion of really planning *what* and *how* you will behave to get to where you want to go. The vast majority of organizations never execute their strategic plans. They determine the mission and guiding principles, and perhaps even the destination points and strategies, but they never link that to actual quarter-by-quarter planning to determine who, when, and what has to get done to get to where you want to go. It is amazing to see beautiful binders in the offices of senior executives with lots of dust on them because they have remained untouched since the "completion" of the strategic plan.

Creating a breakthrough model

It is valuable to begin to think about getting to the destination in manageable steps. The process of noting what you will do broken down by time and the organizational capabilities required to do so forces you to think through how much you can accomplish and in what time frame. Be aggressive, but realistic, with goal-setting. It is demoralizing for everyone when goals are not achieved, and we often discount what it really takes to make the sort of progress we desire.

Key Operating Practice: In addition to noting all the things you will do, note what will be discarded as far as operating practice, processes, and ways of working. There are usually a lot of processes and practices that no longer serve the organization well. Consider what you can get rid of so you can release resources to focus on what you really want.

A client was recently preparing dinner for his family. He got out a large pot roast, cut the end off, and put it in the pan to begin cooking it. His wife walked in and asked why he was cutting off the end of the roast. "Because my mother did it that way," he said. After a pause, he called his mom to ask her why. "Because my mom did it that way," she said. So he called his grandmother. Her response: "I cut off the end because my pot was too small."

An effective goal-setting process is really about change. Effective change depends on employees, leaders, and managers altering how they think, what they believe to be so about the organization, and changing the status quo. To achieve these sorts of adjustments, explicitly outline what will be different in each time period. Consider whether current organizational processes and ways of working are aligned with the goals and strategies or whether they are in the way. In addition, evaluate if you typically get off track easily. Do short-term problems and opportunities frequently preempt longer-term plans and undermine your progress? Who will stay focused on executing the long-term plans and keep others aligned? Is follow-up something you and your organization are generally good at? Are there consequences when commitments are not met?

Don't assume these types of things will change quickly. If your organization is not good at follow-up and people are not generally held accountable, don't design a plan that depends on that changing immediately. You should address these challenges as part of your plan, but try to be realistic. People and cultures don't change quickly. You'll have to work with what you've got for some period of time. Think about and plan for how you can do that well while you are changing things.

Always think through both the *what* and the *how* when it comes to achieving your goals. To assist in truly determining what it will take to get to your destination, the following is a model to support you in outlining each step.

Think through your destination points and compare them to your current state. Based on the gaps between the two, note what you will do **incrementally** different to achieve your goals.

➤ What will happen in the next six months to make progress?

➤ What operating goals and strategies can you achieve in that time frame?

➤ What capabilities must be in place to support getting there?

➤ Consider:

   ❧ How much change can be managed and absorbed productively?

   ❧ What will it really take to increase skills, knowledge, or competency levels?

   ❧ If systems or new processes need to be created, what are the realistic implementation timelines?

What will you do **substantially** different to achieve your goals?

➤ What will happen after the first six months and prior to your first 18 months of progress?

➤ What operating goals and strategies can you achieve in that time frame?

➤ What capabilities must be in place to support getting there?

What will you do that begins to achieve the type of **transformational** goals you set?

➤ What will happen after the first 18 months of progress? (Recognize that you will revisit your goals and update them prior to that time.)

➤ What operating goals and strategies can you achieve in that time frame?

➤ What capabilities must be in place to support getting there?

The following framework is a useful tool to force you to consider how much change you can achieve in what time frames.

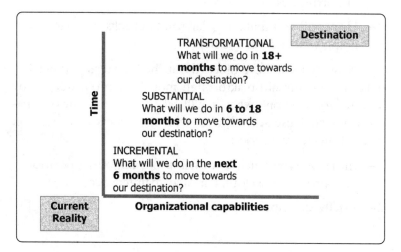

Your breakthrough model outlines what you will do. The focus is on action. Remember that all of the best thought-out plans and goal-setting processes in the world do not make a difference if you do not act on them. Once you have completed your initial draft of your breakthrough model, think through the following:

➤ Does it seem like it will be easy now that you have created your initial plan?

➤ Are you prepared to deal with changes that may become necessary as you execute these plans?

➤ How often have your plans worked out like you intended? How often have your successes happened exactly as you planned?

➤ Does your plan rely on things occurring exactly as you anticipate? What if this does not happen?

➤ Do you have a process for monitoring the marketplace so that you can adjust when necessary?

➤ Is the plan created so that you can take advantage of new market developments, including unexpected opportunities?

➤ How will you make regular reality checks of what is going well and what is not?

Now that you have blocked out the big steps you need to take in your initial breakthrough model, map out quarter by quarter for year one what it will take to get to your destination points. I use spreadsheets with my clients and focus on the following categories:

➤ Initiative type (such as distribution, ongoing operations, new product development, and maintenance).

➤ Briefly describe the initiative.

➤ Place an X under the corresponding quarter in which initiative will be active.

Year 1				Year 2		Year 3	
Q1	Q2	Q3	Q4	1H	2H	1H	2H

➤ Note all direct costs (Cost of Goods).

➤ Estimate total operating expenses required to execute on the initiative.

➤ Note all headcount required to execute including direct, consultants, and contractors.

➤ Input qualitative requirements for any resources outside of your direct organization (who are you depending on to execute?).

➤ Record the impact on your fiscal year results including, revenue, cost savings, and margin.

➤ List any key assumptions made in constructing the initiative.

➤ Note the designated owner or sponsor of the initiative.

Operations plans

The information from your breakthrough modeling is summarized in your one-year operations plan and serves as back-up details for budgeting and such. These plans are typically structured in the following manner:

➤ Overview.

   ❥ Note strategies/areas of focus, and key financial and other goals for fiscal year.

➤ Core Initiatives.

    ❧ Impact, significance to future, strategic value, assumptions, ROI, etc.

➤ Financial Projections.

    ❧ Headcount Plan.

    ❧ Capital Equipment/Expenditures.

    ❧ Key Measures.

How will we get there?

As important as the strategies and operating goals are within the overall framework, they do not stand on their own. How the strategies are achieved is also significant. If the strategies are achieved in a manner that does not create a sustainable organization, the exclusive focus on them has done you a disservice. In other words, it does no good to get to your destination and find you have no one with you because the way you did it destroyed your followers, loyal customers, or other stakeholders in the process.

The focus on exclusively *what* in an organization can be compared to working with a "great" salesperson. For example, your top salesperson surpasses her targets each quarter. She is great in delivering deals and dollars. Unfortunately, she does it by cutting corners, burning bridges with internal resources, and over-promising to customers. No one can stand to be in the same room with her for long. This can't go on indefinitely. The negative consequences will most certainly be felt. And then there is the manager who somehow delivers financial results but has the highest turnover in the organization, whose peers withhold important or helpful information just because it is too painful to deal with him. These are the folks who deliver on performance but do it in such a way that they cause tremendous damage. They take up a lot of management time because you hate to fire them, but you get sick of dealing with them very quickly. They achieve the *what*, but *how* they do it is a compromise of values and/or operating principles. Their motion creates commotion. (See Chapter 4 for how to identify and address this issue.)

Organizations have to be very clear on both *what* and *how* to maintain the appropriate balance and a healthy environment for success.

Defining how you will achieve your strategies and operating goals establishes behavioral parameters for all employees. How you reach your goals has a lasting effect. It is a tough challenge for an organization when someone is achieving goals but doing it in a way that does not align with the values, operating practices, and/or processes the organization desires. (See Chapter 4 for how to align the *how* and the *what* with individuals.)

Go back to your destination points and include more details in this section to include the following:

- What culture (attitudes, beliefs, and behavioral norms) will you aspire to?

- What skills, knowledge, and abilities must exist at the company level?

- What organizational structures will best serve achieving the destination?

- What work processes and metrics will be in place?

- What tools, methods, and technology must be in place to support the organization in achieving the goals?

Going through this step in the process is incredibly important. It forces you to evaluate how realistic and attainable your operating goals are, as well as what it will really take to reach them. For instance, if you have an operating goal that requires a significant increase in sales, but you do not have a sales force in place that has the skills, knowledge, and competencies to achieve this and you are not introducing dramatically improved tools or processes, you must examine how you will realize the goal. You would want to think about how to develop the new skills and competencies required and/or how to acquire them.

I am often astounded that companies I work with want to bypass defining the specifics on *what* and *how*. The most common refrain I hear is that "we're good at just getting things done; somehow it will work out...." It always brings to mind an image of someone driving with his or her eyes closed. Or leaving his or her eyes open but ignoring the gas gauge, the water temperature gauge, the oil pressure gauge, and the speedometer. How crazy! I am convinced these clients initially subscribe to the

> *...and then a miracle happens...*

approach to strategic planning.

You know, the process where you note all the big picture, fancy language stuff to describe nirvana, but you don't quite note all the big steps to get there. Somehow a magic wand is going to wave over the organization, and suddenly you will get to where you want to go even though you don't have the time, dollars, people, or even an idea how!

One of the biggest fallacies of strategic planning and goalsetting is believing that, because you have stated it as a goal, it will magically happen! Do not get caught in this long-standing management trap. Just think back through your own career. How many times did you hear a leader fervently describe where the organization was going and what everyone was going to focus on, only to have it forgotten in a day or so? If you are really brave, go back through your own files and see what you committed to focus on with yourself or your team. Did it happen the way you outlined it? Did you get it done and do it in a way that makes you comfortable you can do it again or leverage what you built? Are you proud of the way you did or did not do it?

Setting goals at the organizational level is valuable and important to align and focus the organization. To assist in linking all employees to the goals, continue your process to the team and individual level.

Team Accountabilities
What do we have to do? How will we do it?

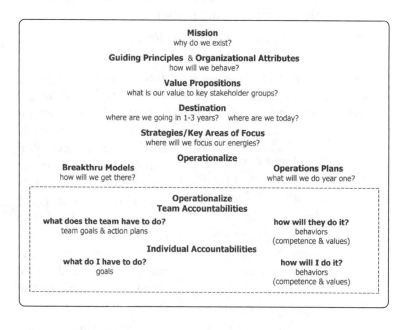

Similar to the process you went through to define the components of the framework at the company level, engage each significant team/division/group within the company to do the same. The basic outline for team/division goal-setting is the same as for the organization. It should cascade from the organizational strategic plan or goals and includes:

- ❧ A Mission Statement (why the particular division or team exists).

- ❧ Guiding Principles or Organizational Attributes (any additions to the company ones if necessary).

- ❧ Value Propositions (the value you have to each of your stakeholder groups both internal and external).

- ❧ Destination Statements (what it looks like when the division or team gets to where they are going within a specified time frame).

- ❧ Strategies (the areas of focus for how the team or division will get there).

A comprehensive process also requires action planning or breakthrough modeling to note what it will really take to get to where you want to go. You have to turn the plan into action and operationalize it. During that process you will determine the *organizational capabilities* necessary at the team and individual level (the required systems, processes, tools, and technology that need to be in place to achieve the strategies).

> Effective leaders and managers have always been about both the results and how you achieve them. Getting to where you are going in a way that supports the overall goals and employees is a much more productive path to travel than the "burn and churn" approach we have seen with some leaders and managers in recent years.

Considering both the *what* and the *how* at the team level is as important as doing it for the company level. The team should have clearly defined operating practices that support the organization's and more clearly define how things get done within the working group.

To conduct a comprehensive team goal-setting process, gather all members of the team and break into small work groups to provide input on each area of the goal-setting model chosen. Have each work group present its ideas and suggestions, and discuss them as a whole team. Delegate a subset of the team to propose the language for the final model.

Individual Goal-Setting
What do I have to do? *How* will I do it?

Individual goal-setting should be a continuous process linked directly to the division or team goals, as well as projects that arise at the team level. There are two important components to individual goals: the *what* and the *how*. The *what* includes the key tasks, milestones, deliverables, and significant activities required, and the *how* includes the competencies, skills, and knowledge necessary to perform well. These two components of individual goals work in concert. Without the competencies, skills, and knowledge required, employees will fail at whatever tasks or deliverables are assigned to them. Without the clarity of tasks or deliverables, all the competencies in the world may not support achieving what is necessary for success. Employees must have clarity on both pieces of the equation.

Spend the time to have each employee clearly define the skills, knowledge, and competencies he or she needs to successfully perform his or her role in the organization, making certain employees link to the organizational accountabilities. This process is sometimes done through the creation of job descriptions, but it should be reviewed following each goal-setting cycle to make sure there is a strong connection between what individuals are expected and rewarded for doing and what the company actually needs in order to achieve success.

Another common fallacy in organizations is having faith that the links between the mission, vision, strategies, and operating goals happen once the company has a written plan. Don't take a chance on this. Without the alignment and focus of each individual employee, the likelihood of achieving company goals is significantly lessened.

Sharing individual goals with the team is a good approach to keeping the team aware of what each team member is focused on. The process of sharing goals can also be used for team members to ask others for assistance or support. Today, unlike 25 years ago, interdependencies with other team members, external partners and suppliers, and customers are common.

Almost the entire organizational goal-setting model is influenced by external forces such as competitors, market conditions, and disruptive technologies, and should be reviewed semiannually to determine if shifts are necessary. The mission should remain constant for an extended period of time even when there are significant external forces, as it defines the very reason the organization exists.

If your organization does not have a clear strategic-planning process or model in place, or the components of one are not concisely laid out, there are a variety of approaches a manager or team leader can take to develop something to work with so that you can cascade goals and link them directly to your team, division, and/or individual direct reports.

➤ Review the previous year's press releases. Look for statements noting who and what the company is as well as where it is heading.

➤ Review any Securities and Exchange Commission documents, including 10-Ks, annual reports, or analysts' reports for information on company direction and strategy.

- Interview company executives.

  - Ask them for their thoughts on the mission and vision of the company.

  - Ask them what the top three priorities are for the year.

  - Ask them what success looks like for the company at the end of the year.

- Read competitive information about your organization, including product reviews, strategy, and speculation regarding the future.

- Attend public presentations by company executives, and make notes on how they describe the organization and where it is headed.

- Ask your direct reports to give you their thoughts and ideas.

- Host a meeting for your peers and colleagues, and gather their input.

- Take notes in the all-company meeting on what the vision is and/or what goals are stated.

- Listen closely to what customers, suppliers, and partners are told about your organization.

- Read marketing materials and/or product literature, including information distributed at conferences or trade shows.

Strategic planning and goal-setting are still incredibly important business processes. They were not practiced in abundance 25 years ago, but there is a greater and greater need to practice them today. Employees today demand the *why*, question their leaders, have more options, and desire inspiration. The basic principle of goal-setting has survived and, although it looks a bit different today and encompasses a broader context of strategic planning, its value is certainly high.

Chapter 1 Executables

➤ Determining the approach for goal-setting that provides the most advantages for the environment you are in is an important first step.

    ❧ Consider the forces affecting the company, such as how much time you have, and use a process that fits with both where you are and where you want to be.

➤ Completing as much of the framework chosen as possible will better support your decision-making and communications.

    ❧ Put in place as many pieces of the organizational goal-setting framework as you can.

    ❧ Answer the core questions: Why do we exist? How will we behave? Where are we going in one to three years? What do we have to do to get there? How will we do it?

➤ Goal-setting is often done at multiple layers within an organization.

    ❧ Work with what you have and what you can influence to affect your area of responsibility as much as possible.

➤ Goals should be aligned from level to level (corporate ➲ team ➲ individual).

    ❧ Even when there are no formal processes for goal-setting at the company-wide level, use the information you can find to do it for your team.

➤ Demonstrating clear links of goals from level to level provides clarity and focus.

    ❧ Create visuals to show the links between teams and the company goals (for example, "Our team produces this so that the company can do this....").

    ❧ Note how goals build from level to level.

➤ Taking an approach that considers both the *what* must be done and the *how* it will get done will keep you aligned with your values and operating principles—one without the other is likely to fail.

  ❧ Clarify, communicate, and respond to *how* and *what* with all employees.

➤ Revisit your goals at least twice a year.

  ❧ Check in often with yourself and others on whether you are living the pieces of the framework.

> Even 25 years ago, effective leaders and managers worked to make it clear to individuals what their responsibilities were and what they would be held accountable for. Business is more complex today, but this basic principle is still incredibly valuable.

Pause for a moment and think about your own goals for the year. Are you clear? Do you have measures in place so you can gauge how you are doing and when to adjust? Have you built the support systems to help yourself?

Chapter 2

Driving Focus: Individual Goal-Setting and Communication

"The problem with communication is the illusion that it is ever achieved."

—Frustrated managers everywhere

Twenty-five years ago, managers sat down with employees and basically gave them tasks to complete. Leaders often provided a level of detail on how to get things done that would feel like micromanagement today. These goal-setting meetings were not about developing understanding of the whole company or where it was headed. They were about getting tasks done in a certain way in a specific time frame. One thing we learned over the past several decades is that this approach can feel demeaning and even childish to employees. It does not engender loyalty or develop others.

Many employees today do not have written goals. There are a lot of reasons for that, including:

❧ Employees get little or no direction to set goals.

❧ The priorities of the company/department/team are constantly shifting, so a belief is formed that goals change so rapidly it would be silly to write them down.

- ❧ Many employees do not realize the importance or impact that setting goals can have for them as well as for the organization.

- ❧ No expectations are established that goal-setting is a part of everyone's job.

- ❧ There is no role-modeling by leaders within the organization.

- ❧ Many employees do not know how to set goals.

- ❧ People fear failure or being criticized if they set goals that are not met (even if it is due to factors well outside their control).

- ❧ Employees may see goal-setting as too complicated or time-consuming.

Goal-setting is an important task that often does not appear urgent. It is easy for it to fall off a to-do list. And with the pace of change today, it is easy to form a belief that, no matter what goal is set, so much will change tomorrow that the goal will be irrelevant. With so much information available, so many possibilities, and so much competing for our time and attention today, goal-setting serves as an incredibly important function in helping us cut through the clutter and focus on what is most important.

> *"Exhaustive studies have shown that only 3% of the population engages in some form of goal setting and only 1% on average write them down. It is no small coincidence that the 1% that write goals down are the highest achieving, highest income earning men and women in the world."*
>
> —Paul Shearstone, expert on sales and time management

Your job as a leader and manager is to address the reasons individuals in your organization do not have written goals, and create a culture where the importance and value of having clear goals is understood and appreciated. The loudest message you can send in this regard is through your own behaviors. Define your own goals, linked to the company strategic framework. Share them with your team. Display them. Talk about them often. Make your expectations about employees' goal-setting explicit. Don't assume employees know how or when to create goals. Provide training and reinforcement so that employees are comfortable learning and practicing goal-setting in a safe environment. Set deadlines so that the task of setting goals moves to the important *and* urgent list.

Employees today want to understand the bigger picture. With four generations in the U.S. workforce today and multiple generations in almost every other country, there are numerous needs that are most effectively met through the goal-setting process. Employees are often motivated and find their work much more interesting if they know how their job fits into the overall scheme of things. It makes for much more interesting chatter at cocktail parties or family events if you can describe your role in terms of its importance and know just what you do (for example, "I am creating a compelling interactive software program that enables our clients to..."). It fills a need most of us have to know that we matter.

Today's workforce has access to global information. Employees get more news in a week than was disseminated in an entire decade a century ago. Those entering the workforce now will change careers (not just jobs) an average of seven times during their professional lifetime! Options abound, and the ongoing search for deeper meaning is important.

In my work with companies of all sizes, employees constantly ask me, "What does this mean? Why are we doing this? Where will this lead us? How is this linked...?" Employees search for answers to uncover the links, and, when they do not find them within the organization, they create ones that seem to fit with the data they have. These made-up answers are almost always inaccurate, incomplete, and negative. It is as if they are writing down the questions after they have the answers. An effective goal-setting process provides the right answers to meet employees' needs and move the organization forward. Goal-setting is not another task to be completed; it is a method for moving forward in the right direction.

Imagine your boss coming to you and asking you to lead a significant project. "Please deliver this product within this time frame and this budget. The product needs to do the following...." What is your first thought? It is probably something along the lines of what most employees think: "Why? How does this contribute to the organization? Where will this take the company? How does it fit within our overall portfolio of offerings? Is this a good move for me in my career?" If you don't get the answers to these questions, you will question the credibility of the request, perhaps even that of your boss. Then, if you are still getting pressure to lead the project, you will make up reasons and answers to the questions so that you can rationalize the purpose and the significance of the project. You know as you go out and engage others to support the effort that they will ask the same questions you did.

> Even with the varied needs and motivators of diverse employees, there are a few things that are consistent across them all:
>
> ► To be included in how what they do links to the overall direction of the company.
> ► To enjoy work.
> ► To have frequent communication including *why* certain projects and priorities are important.

Most goal-setting leaves too much open to individual interpretation and assumption. Without the strategic framework to help fit all the pieces together, we direct others without giving the context for success. Our brains and our hearts require the context. We spend more time working than anything else we do in our lifetimes. For even the older generations at work, work has to have meaning to us, and *our* contributions need to feel valuable for us to perform at our best.

Declare It: Inform Everyone

The first phase of setting individual goals is to communicate and communicate and communicate the strategic planning framework elements broadly. Let's start at the beginning. *Informing* is the most basic step in aligning employees and other stakeholders. Although it is critical that you continue to inform them throughout the year, your initial presentation is important. Your objectives during the informing stage of communication are to update or tell all key audiences of the strategic plan components including the *why*, the *what*, and the *how*. You will also educate all audiences on their roles in meeting the goals and getting to the destination points. To be effective at informing, you should have clarity on the pieces of the strategic framework, including:

- A Mission Statement (why you exist).
- Guiding Principles (how you will behave).
- Value Propositions (what value you have to key stakeholders).
- Destination Points (where you are going in one to three years).
- Strategies (key areas of focus for the entire organization).

Mission
why do we exist?

Guiding Principles & **Organizational Attributes**
how will we behave?

Value Propositions
what is our value to key stakeholder groups?

Destination
where are we going in 1-3 years?   where are we today?

Strategies/Key Areas of Focus
where will we focus our energies?

Imagine explaining the elements of your strategic framework to a school group that knows nothing about your sector or to friends at a cocktail party. If you organize your presentation in this manner, you will be much more successful in communicating the key points. When you communicate initially, do not assume others have the depth of understanding you do. This is one of the most common mistakes I find senior leaders and managers make. They have been thinking about and working on the elements of the strategic planning framework or have participated in a lot of meetings discussing the future of the company, and they assume that with one communication everyone else should be up to speed. It is easy to forget that your perspective as a leader or manager is almost always quite different from the rest of the organization.

If teams in the organization have also already gone through a strategic planning process linked to the organizational one, you may want to share some of the output from the various teams. The more employees understand about the whole organization, the easier it is to see where they fit and how they can contribute to success. If you followed the outline for strategic planning and goal-setting in the previous chapter, you will have almost all of the content you need to be effective and informing. During the inform stage, you are creating the foundation for teams and individuals to develop details on *what* and *how* they will support getting the organization to the destination.

There are many delivery vehicles used to communicate with employees today: e-mail, face-to-face meetings, intranets, letters/mailers, conference calls, and so on. To be most effective in the initial stages of informing, face-to-face meetings are recommended. If you have employees who are geographically dispersed, try to meet with the largest groups face to face, and conduct audio or video conferences to connect others. Use Webinars or other technology that simulate face-to-face interactions. These are some of the most important communications in a company. Spend the time and effort to do them well.

> The tools to communicate have dramatically changed in the past few decades; the need to communicate has not.

Follow up with written communications. I strongly recommend constructing a one-page visual that notes the elements of your strategic plan up to the destination points. Because most of us are visual creatures, having something we can keep in front of us is a powerful tool to keep us focused.

Some of my clients are hesitant about doing this, because they are afraid that a competitor or someone outside the organization will see it. I encourage you to really test this belief. So what if others know why you exist, what behaviors are important to you, or what value you have to others? Those are points that *should* be visible. Sharing them demonstrates pride and confidence in who you are and what you do. It is a funny thing to me when I find clients who think their mission statements should be held closely by those in senior management.

If *why* you exist is a secret to your employees and even to potential employees, individuals are left to fill in the blanks and make up stories. Would you rather employees and customers have clarity on this, or that they fill in the blanks with their own version?

Besides, the illusion of secrecy is dangerous. If your company's success depends on secrecy, rethink who you are and what you do. The ease of spreading information today through e-mail, employee or user group blogs, instant messaging, and short job tenure means that information is going to get out. The irony is that what gets disseminated quickly is not usually what we want communicated. And remember, when there is a void of information, people are left to create their own stories, which are often far removed from the data and usually much more negative than the truth. Take advantage of the natural curiosity of your employees by providing them with the information they need to be successful. Fill in as many blanks as possible so that the story shared is the one that serves the organization and all employees well.

Details of your destination points might need to be held a little more closely than the other elements of your plan. These should be the factors that are creating your competitive advantage, so sharing them too broadly could undermine your organization. You should, however, share the big-picture view of your destination points. Remember that the whole purpose of creating them is to get clarity on what it looks like to get to where you want to go. You want each employee to have this view of the future. It will assist in driving daily behaviors. Share team-specific destination details at a team level, as this will drive the details necessary in goal-setting.

Getting clarity on the destination points throughout the organization creates a decision framework within departments and teams, and among individuals. If we go back to our travel brochure analogy, informing employees of the destination points helps them make a decision between purchasing a train ticket or a plan ticket (and this could make a huge difference if you are planning a vacation across the ocean!). It helps individuals make more decisions that are moving the organization in the right direction without having to constantly check in with their manager.

Think about the number of decisions most employees make on a daily basis. What criteria are your employees currently using to make those decisions? Does the criteria align with where you want the company to go?

Your initial presentation

Structure your initial presentation to provide details and answers. Start with the big picture. Present the mission statement and answer the question "why do we exist?" This is an inspirational statement that should be presented in the future, active tense, as if you are already doing it or being it. Look back through the examples provided in Chapter 1 to see how some of the world's most successful organizations define their reason for being.

> **Key Operating Practice:**
> Forcing yourself to write and present information in the future, active tense directs your mind to the end state. It sets you up for success. Similar to the way an Olympic athlete imagines setting a new world record, stating your mission, vision, and values as if you are already there keeps a powerful image in your mind for focus and energy.

Follow with statements defining how you will behave. Include the guiding principles, organizational attributes, and/or values you defined in your process. Again, present these statements in a future, active tense, as if you

are already behaving this way. Disclose that you are presenting these behaviors in future tense and will discuss some key
actions to address any areas that need attention. You do not
want employees to feel you are removed from reality or mis-
informed about the current state. Your job is to create an
image in the minds of employees of what excellence looks
like while acknowledging that there may be work to do to get
there. This focuses the minds of employees on a positive image versus one where an individual is examining or judging
all that is wrong today.

To help further clarify behaviors, you may want to supple-
ment the definitions of what excellence looks like with statements about what is out of bounds or inappropriate. Giving this
level of detail empowers employees to hold themselves and others more accountable to the desired state. Keep the communication about what is inappropriate within the context of what
excellence looks like so that you keep the minds of employees
focused on a positive set of behaviors. When you say to someone, "Don't think about a pink elephant," the first thing he or
she thinks about is a pink elephant. So present the definition of
desired behaviors (both what is and what is not desired) while
creating a positive image in the minds of your audience.

For example, if one of your guiding principles is that all
employees act with integrity, define excellence. You might
say, "consistently conducts themselves in an honest and trustworthy manner, does not pursue their own individual objectives to the detriment of company goals or others, sets an
example for others to follow, and does the right thing."

You would then communicate behavioral indicators or examples of what an employee looks like when he or she is acting
with integrity. Indicators might include: responds honestly and
directly to inquiries, keeps confidences, consistently treats others with dignity and respect, respectfully questions behaviors
when they do not align with the values of the organization,

presents the unvarnished truth in an appropriate and helpful manner, puts the total organization first, and is a role model for others in living all the values of the company.

Once you have created a clear picture of excellence, mention some examples of behaviors that are not acceptable or contraindicators to acting with integrity. These might include: does not take a stand or hedges on answers, treats others indifferently, is inconsistent (does one thing but says another), exhibits questionable ethics by doing things that always need further explanation, takes credit for work done by others, and blames others for own mistakes.

Do not end with the contraindicators. Remember the pink elephant? We want employees to have the image of what excellence looks like in their heads, so, after you have presented details on all your organizational attributes or values, recap with the desired state—leave individuals with a clear image of excellence.

Now, talk about where you are going—your destination and why it is the best place to go. Share as much as you can in the following areas:

- Where the organization needs to go and why.
- Business justification.
- Customer needs.
- Industry demands/trends.
- Internal efficiencies.
- What it will look like when we get there.
- The advantages/benefits of this decision, including your value propositions.
- Any possible disadvantages (be candid and direct if there are)—uncertainties, constantly changing marketplace, and unknown customer progression.

Once you have shared the destination points, narrow the focus back in to discuss the core strategies. Each employee should be able to link what he or she is doing to at least one of the core strategies. If someone cannot link his or her goals and activities to the strategy, it is a good indicator that he or she is working on the wrong things. Present what you believe the organization has to do to continue/regain/maintain success. Note the core strategies including key measures for each one. Pause and discuss why these are the strategies. As you are preparing your thoughts on the *why*, force yourself to consider the different perspectives of your audience. Speak to the needs of as many different audience members as you can.

Next, share how the organization will work on the strategies and get to the destination. Describe what culture will be required; what skills, knowledge, and abilities must exist in the company; what structures will best support the organization; what processes and metrics will be in place; what tools, methodologies, and technology will be required.

Again, pause and consider what all of this might mean to employees. Try to present from the perspective of *What difference does this make to me/my job/my team?* For groups, teams, or roles, provide as much detail as possible about what is changing—what no longer will be done, what no longer will exist, what possibilities there are (specific or sample projects). In addition, share your expectations on how you want individuals to behave differently. Present using positive behavioral examples. Share the details of what excellence looks like in terms of behaviors, not what people are doing wrong. Consider what knowledge or belief individuals must have to behave differently. Also think about what you are sharing as it relates to career development or opportunities for employees.

In addition to sharing your vision of what will be, identify key things that will not be changing. It is important for individuals to have a sense of stability, continuity, and identity to the group. Adults typically get comfortable with *what is*, even if they are complaining about it!

To build additional rapport with your audiences and relate to individuals more effectively, describe what the new destination, along with all its components, means to you as the leader. Acknowledge what you believe some of the feelings and thoughts of the audience members must be (for example, "I know this is part of our constant change and that sometimes change can wear us out..."). Predict and discuss some of the negative aspects that can be expected, such as interpersonal reaction to constant change, internal systems confusion, and client transitions.

Incorporate the following details into your presentation as well. Share the timeline (from your breakthrough model). Mention when significant efforts or projects will happen. Discuss the stages of significant efforts. Share how employees (and customers or others) will be kept informed during these stages.

If significant change will occur, provide details on transitioning, including how client interactions will be handled, what types of discussions with other employees should take place and when they should happen, and the type of support that will be provided (people, technology, and coaching). Share who is responsible for specifics and provide information on who to go to with questions, ideas, or concerns.

Provide as many details as possible regarding implementation. What do you need employees to do, what will leaders do, and by when? Reiterate how people will be kept informed and where to go for answers.

Finally, end your session with a "thank you." Sincerely thank everyone for their ongoing energy, enthusiasm, and commitment. Encourage people to ask questions or raise concerns with their immediate managers.

Whew! This communication thing seems like a lot. It is, and it isn't. If you consider what is at stake, this initial communication is very little effort for a huge return. Consider the decisions that get made throughout your organization on a daily basis. Ponder the number of client or customer interactions and how much opportunity there is for something to be said that does not align with where you want things to go. Spending the time and energy up front to get all employees aligned is well worth the effort. The return on investment is high. You will be enabling ongoing decision-making and appropriate interactions that all contribute in a positive way to moving things forward. You will empower individuals to determine goals and tasks that are aligned. You will create expectations of excellence that almost everyone will want to live up to. (After all, how many employees come to work in the morning thinking, "I really want to do a crappy job today"?)

Almost all of us want to do the right thing. We want to help the organization succeed. We want to see our colleagues do well, our customers satisfied, and our products or services deliver. Give employees the tools to achieve excellence. You will be amazed at how they will deliver!

Speaking of tools, let's continue on the communication journey.

Following a company or team meeting, you may want to provide your employees with a brochure (hard copy and/or online) or other document that summarizes what you shared. Remember, most of us are visual creatures, so the more visual reinforcement you can create for employees, the more likely they are to remain focused and aligned. The following is an outline for a "What we need to do and why?" tri-part brochure template.

Inside flap (when open)	Back	Front flap
Guiding principles Organization attributes Values	Who to contact for more information or if there are any questions	XXX Company Year Logo Why we exist—the mission statement
Left flap (when open)	**Middle flap (when open)**	**Right flap (when open)**
Destination statements	What and How Strategies with timelines	What this means to me and my team (worksheet-type format for notes and action items)

Team communication

In addition to ongoing company-wide communications, messaging needs to cascade so teams and individuals get the level of detail necessary to make good decisions in their roles. Once employees have been informed at the company-wide level, conduct team meetings. Provide a summary of the information presented to the whole company. Each manager or team leader should pause and consider what all of this might mean to employees at the team level. As noted earlier, each manager should work to present from the perspective of *What difference does this make to me/my job/my team?* Within the team, provide as much detail as possible about what is changing— what will no longer be done, what will no longer exist, what possibilities there are (specific or sample projects).

Similar to the company-wide meeting, managers should identify key things that will not be changing. Use examples that apply directly to the team. Talk to specific projects, customers, processes, and so forth as much as possible. If you can provide comfort to employees through demonstrating some stability and continuity of what is already working well, employees are more likely to trust you and work with the changes versus against them.

During significant change, I often coach clients to honor and respect the past while creating the future. After all, the company is not a complete failure. If you overemphasize all of the changes that are needed, you insult those people who have been in the organization for years. There are usually a great deal of positive things that can be mentioned that got the organization to where it is today. Talented individuals show up each day and they do so even with all of the choices available, so make sure to communicate the positives from the past while you are communicating how great the future will be.

And even if you think these things are obvious, say them anyway. Your explicit acknowledgment of all the goodness from the past will often help those who are a little reluctant to change.

Go through the guidance provided for conducting an effective company-wide meeting and apply it at the team

Key Operating Practice: There are many companies that post their missions, visions, and values. Posting them is great only if you are really working toward them and behaving in a manner that aligns with them. Otherwise, it is much worse to so visibly state you are doing one thing when another is quite clearly going on.

level. Make sure to link everything to the team and to yourself so that the message is authentic. At the team level, you may also want to discuss any inter-team dependencies (how will you work with those you need to, including external teams such as suppliers and vendors). Focus on any expectations of new behaviors and new ways of operating on the team, and provide specifics on how certain roles are different now from what they were in the past. Ask team members for their thoughts. Some great questions for a manger to pose to the team are: What are you reactions? What are the implications for our team? What are the advantages? What concerns do you have? What would you like to know more about?

Seek commitment from the team as a whole, and then in follow-up meetings, from each individual. Ask for the current level of commitment to the team success. If it is low, ask what it will take to increase it.

Following your initial presentations and team meetings, you will want to keep the information you shared visible and accessible. You cannot stop at just the introductory meetings with one follow-up piece. Too much competes for our attention these days. Employees (just like leaders and managers) can get off track easily. We seek what we know and what is comfortable, so you have to constantly provide a compelling vision for others to move toward it.

> Communicating about goals as outlined in *The One Minute Manager* 25 years ago still makes sense today:
> - ➤ Review goals frequently.
> - ➤ Take a minute every once in a while to consider *how* goals are being achieved.
> - ➤ Check to make sure behaviors align with the values and operating practices of the organization.
> - ➤ Support realignment of behaviors when necessary.

The leader's and manager's job is to consistently support informing, inspiring, and engaging employees in what needs to be done and how. Communicating strategies and goals once is standard practice in most organizations that have them. Unfortunately, clarity of where and how an organization will achieve its goals is highly unlikely to be achieved in a single communication. Tests have shown that immediately after listening to a 10-minute oral presentation, the average listener has heard, understood, properly evaluated, and retained approximately half of what was said. And, within 48 hours, that drops off another 50 percent to a final 25 percent level of effectiveness. In other words, we quite often comprehend and retain only one-quarter of what was said. This compounds the problem when you consider how heavily we rely on the spoken word as a method of communication. After one presentation, the likelihood of anyone having clarity on organization strategies and goals is very small. Only through constant communication delivered in a variety of formats can we hope to create alignment, understanding, and commitment.

Study after study confirms that productivity and employee commitment are highest in those work areas where people are kept fully and regularly informed. The better you communicate, the better your return on investment. Organizations that communicate effectively outpace organizations that don't. According to a global Watson Wyatt study with more than 267 companies representing all major industry sectors, a significant improvement in communication effectiveness is associated with a 29.5 percent increase in market value. In addition, companies that communicate effectively were more likely to report employee turnover rates below those of their industry peers.

Although some of the information needs of employees are met through electronic or written communications, surveys show that employees place a greater value on face-to-face communication by a long shot, especially when it comes from the person for whom they work. Studies show that only 7 percent of what employees hear is through the actual words used. Body language and behavior communicate 55 percent of the message, and 38 percent is communicated in tone and inflection. Although we have created emoticons and other visual cues to assist with infusing "body language" into electronic and printed communications, it is still the manager or supervisor, face to face, who is the preferred source of information. Unfortunately, many employees don't feel that their bosses communicate effectively with them. This dissatisfaction frequently snowballs into lack of trust, mediocre effort, increased turnover, and disengagement from the goals and objectives of the company.

In a major study on employee job satisfaction conducted by the Society for Human Resource Management and CNNfn, three factors related to communication placed in the top eight of 22 very important job satisfaction factors:

❧ Relationship with immediate supervisor.

❧ Communication between employees and senior management.

❧ Management recognition of employee job performance.

Nine out of 10 employees said that the effectiveness of communication is a very important influencer in overall job satisfaction and productivity.

Set up a system to remind managers to discuss goals and the strategic planning framework elements with employees on a regular basis. Provide tools and templates managers and team leaders can use in monthly team meetings and in one-on-one conversations.

To complement this face-to-face communication, develop some creative ways to keep information in front of everyone. Change it up each month so individuals continue to see it.

Include elements of the strategic planning framework in news-letters, e-mail messages, on your intranet, and within presentations used at team and company meetings. You should also have a plan to provide new hires with the information. Consider how you can highlight the goals periodically. Can you create posters for the employee break rooms? Do you have an intranet that is often accessed by employees? If so, how can you use it to keep the goals visible? Do you have a monthly e-mail message you send to employees? If so, how can you embed the goals in it each time to keep everyone in sync? Get creative. Put your mission and values on notepads, paper cubes, and/or mouse pads. Think about things employees use every day, and use those as your communication vehicles. For those components of your strategic framework that may change more frequently (such as strategies and operating metrics), make sure to update employees each time there is a change, including details on why things changed.

I have helped clients develop tent cards for the cafeteria tables, posters for public areas in the offices, paycheck stuffers, intranet homepages, screen savers, note cubes, and so on. There is almost no limit to simple things you can do to communicate the most important messages in the company. And these are messages that, like many others, cannot be overcommunicated.

The inform phase is all about making sure each and every employee knows the basics of your organization and/or team goals. The most frequent mistake made is to do a once-a-year communication and then go silent on updates. Things change frequently in business today. When changes occur that affect goals, measures, and how you will get things done, communicate again. I have yet to experience an organization that overcommunicated about goals. Instead, we start running and, in our busy-ness, forget that others aren't privy to all we are exposed to. When a change does become evident and employees have not been informed, they are much more likely to fill the void with negative information, which is typically far worse than the truth. Pausing to communicate frequently will save you hours in addressing myths, half-truths, and just plain inaccurate information.

During the team and company meetings, set the tone for openness, mutual understanding, and respect. Don't try to force closure on the initial discussion. Ensure that team members have future opportunities to discuss and process information. Remember that you have probably had several months to consider and digest everything in the strategic framework, but this is the first time many employees will have heard them. Create a process for employees to ask questions a few days following the initial presentation.

Put Me in Coach: Create Individual Goals
What do I have to do, and *how* will I do it?

Teams and employees must have a foundation on which to build individual goals. Trying to conduct goal-setting without having a strategic framework in place is like trying to put windows in a house that is not constructed yet. As mentioned in Chapter 1, even if there is no formal strategic plan available, work to construct the basics from other sources so that you have a frame on which to build.

Individual goal-setting should be a continuous process linked directly to the division or team goals as well as projects that arise at the team level. There are two important components to individual goals: the *what* and the *how*. The *what* includes the key tasks, milestones, deliverables, and significant activities required, and the *how* includes the competencies, skills, knowledge, and behaviors necessary to perform well. These two components of individual goals work in concert. Without the competencies, skills, and knowledge required, employees will fail at whatever tasks or deliverables are assigned to them. Without the clarity of tasks or deliverables, all the competencies in the world may not support achieving what is necessary for success. Employees must have clarity on both pieces of the equation.

There are hundreds of books and tools to help you with the specifics of individual goal-setting. There are also fairly ubiquitous approaches outlining details of what should be included in individual goals. Later in this chapter, I will provide some guidance on the details of individual goal-setting and leave it to you to choose a specific process/system/tool that works best for you and your organization. The details of exactly how you do it are not nearly as important as doing something that fits the overall strategy of the organization with the everyday work of individuals.

Many organizations conduct individual goal-setting annually. It is an area that has grown rapidly in the past few years as online tools have become more sophisticated. There are some excellent tools available. It is always funny to me to consult with those companies that have spent thousands of dollars implementing a system or process to drive individual goals, but that cannot articulate the mission, the guiding principles, the value propositions, the strategies, or the destination points. Employees in these organizations are required to dream up goals and tasks based on their interpretation of where the company is headed and what is important. It is an expensive guessing game with the company's success at stake.

I worked with one client recently who utilizes a company-wide system for goal-setting. The senior management actually reviews the goals of the entire organization annually. They are confounded every year when the goals of individuals often do not seem linked to the plans of the company, and it requires hours of time to redo the goals. They send dozens of e-mails back and forth, and meet with team leaders repeatedly to refine the projects that will get the resources. Despite a great deal of encouragement and coaching, they have yet to implement ongoing communications to share the strategic plan to alleviate the misalignment. The senior executives work on the strategic framework for weeks and weeks, and then assume everyone fully understands it after one employee meeting. Better to keep doing it over than do it right from the start, I guess!

Spend the time to have each employee clearly define what needs to get done and how it will get done in their individual roles. Individuals should note the tasks or significant responsibilities of the job and then the skills, knowledge, and competencies they need to successfully perform their roles in the organization. All of these elements should link to the team *what* and *how* as well as the company *what* and *how*. This process is sometimes initially done through the creation of job descriptions, but it should be reviewed following each goal-setting cycle to make sure there is a strong connection between what individuals are expected and rewarded for doing and what the company actually needs to achieve success.

I am often surprised at the disconnect with the criteria we use to hire people and then manage them, and then promote or terminate them. It often looks like it all comes from different companies instead of a simple set of clear criteria outlining what excellence looks like for each role. Become clear on what excellence looks like in your organization, and you will find it amazingly helpful to use this in all the other people processes—staffing, promotion, compensation, and so on.

Following are categories typically found in an effective goal-setting process for individuals:

➤ What do I need to achieve?

- ❧ Key performance objectives.
- ❧ Roles/responsibilities.
- ❧ Major tasks and goals.

➤ This goal is:

  ❧ **Specific:** We can define it so that we both are clear on what it looks like when it is being done and/or completed.

  ❧ **Measurable:** We know what success looks like in quantitative and/or qualitative terms.

  ❧ **Attainable:** It can be done even if it is a stretch.

  ❧ **Relevant:** The goal links to the team, company goals, and strategic framework.

  ❧ **Time-bound:** It has clear deadlines and/or milestones. This distinguishes ongoing tasks and job responsibilities as part of the job definition, but not necessarily in the goals each year.

    ➤ SMART goal-setting was originally developed by the U.S. military. It was popularized during the 1980s by numerous individuals and has been written about in thousands of publications. There are several variations on definitions and acronyms used. Define the criteria for goals in a way that works in your organization.

➤ How will I achieve it?

  ❧ Competencies, skills, and knowledge required.

➤ Tracking sources and timeline.

➤ Why this goal supports moving us closer to our destination.

So that you have a clear place to note the results at the end of the cycle:

➤ Actual results.

Another common fallacy in organizations is having faith that the links between the mission, vision, strategies, and operating goals happen once the company has a written plan.

Don't take a chance on this. Without the alignment and focus of each individual employee, the likelihood of achieving your goals is significantly lessened. By adding the section—why this goal supports moving us closer to our destination—to the individual goal-setting process, you will create a place for individuals to think through and document how their individual goals link to the destination points for the team (which, of course, link directly to the destination points for the company). Forcing this closes the loop. Without it, you might assume there is understanding and a clear link for each individual. Why leave that to chance?

Twenty-five years ago it was fairly simple to create specific goals that remained the same for months—even years. Organizations were expected to run like clockwork and were designed mechanically with every piece in its place. Today, the level of specificity can be decreased somewhat if you consider the needs of most employees to have flexibility in managing priorities (inside and outside of work), schedules, and details of how it gets done. As long as the *how* a goal is achieved falls within the values or operating principles of the organization, allowing differences in approach is a healthy management style. Initiative and creativity are valued in most workplaces today, and there is no reason to eliminate them from goal-setting as long as the end state or destination is clear.

The most important outcome of the individual goal-setting is a commitment from the employee based on shared understanding.

Sharing individual goals with the team is a good approach to keeping the team aware of what each member is focused on. The process of sharing goals can also be used for team members to ask others for assistance or support. Today, unlike 25 years ago, interdependencies with other team members, with external partners and suppliers, and with customers are common. There are very few jobs left that function without significant interaction with others.

Almost the entire organizational goal-setting model is influenced by external forces such as competitors, market conditions, and disruptive technologies, and should be reviewed semiannually to determine if shifts are necessary. The mission should remain constant for an extended period of time even when there are significant external forces, as it defines the very reason the organization exists.

Communicating goals clearly and consistently follows the process of actually creating a strategic plan and setting goals as one of the most important jobs for a leader or manager. After all, goals that are forgotten or misunderstood have little impact, or, worse, lead employees to focus on the wrong things. And goals can quickly be forgotten in the day-to-day chaos of our everyday jobs.

The reality of the 21st-century workplace is that communication about company strategies, goals, values, and operating principles is a lot more than a "nice thing to do." It's a powerful tool for competitive advantage. It drives business performance and is a key contributor to organizational success.

Cheer Me On: Help Me Become Enthusiastic

Inspiring communications

In your initial presentation of goals, you will have inspired employees by sharing a compelling vision of what tomorrow and success looks like. It is now time to focus more on how to keep employees excited and energized about achieving the goals. To further inspire employees, constantly discuss the aspirational components of your model.

Over time, share why you believe your destination is compelling. Periodically ask others why they want to go there with you. Ask for ideas and input on how to get there as effectively as possible. Share why you believe it is a great destination. Articulate how it reflects the unique characteristics your company offers—what you can be the very best at.

Always discuss the goals with enthusiasm. Talk about what they mean to you personally. Solicit similar input from others and share it via e-mails, via the intranet, or in quarterly company meetings. The more you get others talking about what it means to them individually, the more likely you are to attain buy-in and commitment. It is okay to be a little anxious about achieving all the goals. After all, if it were going to be easy, you are probably not stretching enough to achieve what is nearly possible.

> **Key Operating Practice:** When you communicate clearly and listen effectively, people know what's expected. And they know that their needs and ideas count. When people feel this way, they are more likely to cooperate and eventually buy in.

Bring the impact/value of your company to life by sharing customer feedback. Note how you have made a difference in the world/your community/your clients. If possible, create a video of customer interviews and share it with all employees. Invite a customer to present at a company meeting. Present samples from written testimonials you have received. Make it real by sharing stories and information about individuals affected.

If possible, simulate the end state of one of your goals. You could create a mock newspaper with a headline announcing your major achievement or an award. Note what it means to the company, the community, employees, and so on. In the articles, outline how you got to the destination (reiterating the *how* in your model).

Celebrate achieving milestones. Send thank-you notes to employees. Host a celebration event that brings employees together and is high energy. Use music, visuals, handouts, and giveaways to maintain momentum and enthusiasm.

Continue to note when new barriers or challenges have arisen that slowed down progress or forced you to change strategies or direction. Employees want the truth, and will trust leaders and managers who share both the good and bad news. Share as much information as you can on an ongoing basis.

Check in periodically and ask yourself, "Are my messages and communications...

❧ aspirational?"

❧ compelling?"

❧ comprehensive?"

❧ challenging?"

❧ honest?"

❧ two-way?"

Keeping the destination in front of employees keeps the energy about it positive. It is so easy to get lost in the day to day and stew in all the reasons you won't get to where you want to go. Your role as a leader or manager is to make sure there is a balance of focus on day-to-day tasks and long-term achievements. There is a lot going on today that fights against you in achieving this balance. We are moving at a pace that does not allow a lot of time for reflection or contemplation. We are struggling to answer all the e-mails, attend all the meetings, and actually do some "real work" as well. By making time to keep the destination and other components of your strategic framework on each employee's radar, you will have taken a big step toward maintaining the inspiration required to achieve great things.

There will be days when this too seems like just another task on your own list. Remember, there are few tasks as important as this one, even though it does not always appear as urgent. When individuals and teams are focused and moving in the right direction, you might be surprised at what falls off your own to-do list.

Keep Me Connected: Forge Links
Engaging behaviors

Keep employees engaged in achieving the goals throughout the year by revisiting them and asking about progress. Once you have gone through individual goal-setting, first check to make sure all individual goals are linked to the company goals. If individuals and/or teams have difficult linking to the strategies, work to make sure the strategies are more understandable. Keep the language simple and to the point. Be sure that individuals are clear on both the *what* and the *how* for their teams as well as for themselves.

Share stories of how teams are aligned and achieving goals. Highlight team accomplishments and link them each time to the strategy they support. Highlight operating principles and values as well so that they are continually viewed as important. Ask team members to present a quick story or anecdote on something from the organizational goals at each team meeting.

> **Key Operating Practice:** Treat change as you would any other business initiative. Don't discount how tough change is for employees (and yourself) and don't underestimate the energy you must commit to deal with it effectively.

Create an employee pledge wall or flipchart where employees can note their commitment to achieving the goals by signing it or noting one thing they will do differently to support the goals. The more you can have employees physically do something that demonstrates their commitment to and engagement with the goals, the better.

Measure your progress of employee understanding, commitment, inspiration, and engagement. Take quick surveys following team and/or company meetings. Solicit questions via e-mail or your intranet, and note what questions are asked. Address the questions in employee forums as much as possible based on the premise that, if one person is asking, many may have the same questions or concern. Openly thank employees for asking questions or raising concerns.

Ask yourself, "Are the ongoing messages...

- ❥ understandable?"

- ❥ appealing?"

- ❥ presenting the goals as achievable and aspirational?"

- ❥ stimulating?"

Consider if your behaviors demonstrate that goals are critical to the company's success. What are you doing (not just saying) on an ongoing basis that would demonstrate to employees how important individual and team goals are? I often assess individual leaders as well as entire organizations on the intended and unintended messages being sent through the behaviors of the leaders. I typically find managers who schedule one-on-one meetings to discuss goals only to cancel or reschedule them numerous times. What does this say to employees? It usually says

I have other things that are much more important than discussing your goals with you.

And it says it loudly. So loudly, in fact, that I cannot hear when you tell me something different. I have observed leaders who cannot tell you the company strategies or the progress toward achieving objectives. What does this say to employees? It says

These things are not important. Just do what I say when I say it.

And it says it loudly. As a leader or manager, remember that your behavior speaks volumes! Your words are very quiet when it comes to what you say is important, what is valued, and what will be rewarded.

Changes

When goals or strategies need to change during the year, and they will, keep in mind some basic change management principles.

Establish your commitment to the change by determining what you have at stake and why. Determine the audiences, both internal and external, affected or with a need to know. Communicate changes as broadly as possible. Even if you do not think a team or individual is directly affected, you may not realize there are processes or interactions that will be affected.

Think through and consider things that are critical to success, and therefore a diversion from them has serious consequences. Decide and note these absolutes (open-door approach, honesty, raising issues quickly, and so on).

Determine who is sponsoring the change. This is the individual or team that has responsibility for the change and the authority to make decisions. Also determine who needs to actively support the change through actions such as communications, follow-up, and measuring. Make sure you set the expectations with sponsors and direct supporters. Don't assume they understand what excellence looks like for these roles or that they have a clear picture of the new end state. Spend the time to define excellence up front. It will save you countless hours later.

Develop the story you will tell about the change. Be honest and candid. Communicate what has happened, providing as much information as possible (remember that employees will always fill in the blanks with negative stories, so give as much detail as possible while focusing on the positive). Then tell employees what is next. Cover where the organization needs to go and why, including business justification, customer needs, industry demands/trends, internal efficiencies, what it will now look like when you get there, and so on.

You will also want to talk about the advantages and benefits of the change. Address implementation specifics, especially timing, noting how people will be kept informed throughout the process. Tell employees what they are responsible for, including employee next steps and to do's. Describe the support (for example, people, technology, and assistance) that will be provided.

Of course, communicate early and often, and work hard to continue to listen throughout. Balance the focus and type of communications you use. Do approximately 80 percent two-way, face to face, briefings, conversations, and so on, and 20 percent "long life" (that is, intranets, e-mail, and hard copies, such as brochures and handouts).

> **Key Operating Practice:**
> Manage communications tightly over the months (don't lose focus). New stories will be made up to fill in any gaps that evolve after the initial communication, and the made-up stories are typically much more negative than any truths.

Manage the signals being sent throughout the organization. Think about and consider what each leader will do to signal what is and what is not important in the new organization. Eliminate negative signals quickly by clarifying the intention of the behavior and stating what is expected.

Use credible communicators in the organization. You don't have to stick with formal leaders. Try using informal thought leaders to get out your desired messages. In an organization I led, we used "enhancement enthusiasts"—individual thought leaders who could influence others. We met with the group weekly, shared information directly, and encouraged them to ask tough questions of the leaders. They shared with us what and where they thought resistance would occur. We strongly encouraged them to talk to others. The interactions with these thought leaders was going to happen anyway, so we felt that, by providing information and support, the messages communicated would be much more positive. This approach was a complement to preparing managers with as much information as possible. A combination of these actions served the company very well, and the significant reorganization of the entire company almost seemed like a nonevent three months later.

In addition to measuring the success of the change in terms of goals, measure your communication process and progress by checking for awareness (look for evidence in the form of behavior and words) and testing for understanding (ask questions; query the employees on specifics).

As a manager, you will be depended on even more during change. The single greatest factor in retaining employees is the manager. You need to be informative, supportive, and encouraging by helping the team understand that transition is natural, even if uncomfortable. You will also want to continuously communicate about what's happening, providing as much clarity as possible and even stating that nothing has changed since the last communication, if that is the case. Create temporary

systems/roles/policies/processes, if necessary. Clearly identify your expectations and short-term results (deadlines, required results, and desired behaviors). Remain visible,
available, and openly supportive of the change, and allow the
team to vent in the appropriate forums without repercussion.
Identify resistance to change and address issues as quickly as
possible, with sensitivity. At the same time, continually focus
on the future destination and ask for commitment to it.

During change, it is advisable for managers to re-recruit
key team members. Get them invested in the change. Recognize and reward desired behaviors quickly, often, and informally as well as formally. Continue to support development
for employees and yourself.

Be Great: Become an Excellent Communicator

This section outlines some general tips on effectively communicating about goal-setting.

> **Key Operating Practice:**
> Be honest as both a giver
> and as a receiver of
> information.

State if what you are ex-
pressing is based on fact or assumption. Sometimes we get
very excited about our topic
and forget that we are speaking in absolutes. Even when
you think it is common
knowledge, let others know that you are open to suggestion
or input, or that you are stating your opinion. Try to check in
with your employees on their knowledge of the topic or situation instead of assuming that they already know.

Shoot straight with employees if the goals you are discussing with them are negotiable or not. Note if your comments are open for discussion. You don't want to engage in a
conversation with employees who believe that they have input
if that is not really the case. There may be times when a goal is
mandated from others or because of an extreme situation with

a customer, for instance. If this is the case, just discuss it openly with the employees. You may need to allow them to vent or express frustration or concern, but at least you will not mislead them and create a feeling of betrayal.

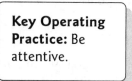

Key Operating Practice: Be attentive.

Particularly when you are being more directive about some goals, remain attentive when the employee is speaking. Try to stay focused on his or her concerns or input. Anytime you are in a conversation and realize that you stopped listening for a moment, admit it. "Sorry. I just got distracted. Could you go over that again please?"

To demonstrate your attentiveness, face the speaker. Try to stay focused on the speaker while he or she is talking instead of preparing a response or thinking about other things. One way to keep your mind occupied is to demonstrate you are listening by commenting on what the other person has been saying. Ask for elaboration on points about which you are unclear. Use open language, such as "help me understand...." Another way to demonstrate your attentiveness is to describe what you think from the point of view of the speaker. You can also demonstrate your interest in the speaker by picking up on a point he or she makes and expanding on it further.

When you are speaking, watch the listeners' body language to see if it appears they have become disinterested or distracted. Stop talking when you see an individual is distracted and check in with him. Re-engage your listeners by asking them if they agree with you or have additional data or a different perspective. Frequently check to see that you are being understood by asking for feedback and insight. Remember to truly ask instead of pretending to ask. In other words, "Don't you agree?" is pretending to ask. "What do you think?" is really asking.

Always work to allow your listener to finish his or her point without interrupting (unless he or she is rambling or

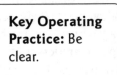

Key Operating Practice: Be polite.

there really is an urgent situation requiring immediate action). If possible, write down any point that makes you want to interrupt, and then refocus and continue listening for more information.

In goal-setting, it is appropriate to express your ideas even when they differ from those around you, but don't get upset when someone disagrees with you. Begin by acknowledging what the other person has said, and state that you disagree because.... Try to expose your thinking about the topic or area, and check in as you are stating your own opinion or belief. Remember, however, that, if the goal is not negotiable for some reason, you should state so after listening, and acknowledge the disagreement.

Key Operating Practice: Be clear.

Especially when you are communicating about sensitive topics or things you are fairly certain your listener will disagree with, choose your words carefully and precisely so that what you say is what you mean to say. Avoid overreactions, exaggerations, and generalizations. Steer clear of statements that may be interpreted as personal to minimize defensiveness. Describe things as you perceive them to be without making any judgment about them. Use words that are simple to understand and in common usage. In goal-setting, it is critical that you gain shared understanding, commitment, and buy-in to the goals, so these practices are particularly important.

When goal-setting with your team, ask employees if they are clear and can restate the goal. Ask if there are barriers to achieving the goal and in what areas they need support. Ask clarifying questions if you are unsure of the employee's view, but try hard not to get defensive or too directive. Ask the employee if there are other goals he or she thinks are critical to success, and try to incorporate those as well.

When initially constructing goals, ask your peers and others in the organization for input into your own goals as well as those for your team. Ask a customer, if you have that luxury. Try to remain open and truly inquisitive about both what others

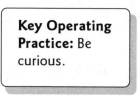

Key Operating Practice: Be curious.

think you should focus on and why. As you are seeking input from diverse sources, including your direct reports, provide your perspective. Ask for your listener's opinion about things that you have said.

Adopt a perspective that looks at the whole situation, especially when discussing goals (both your own and others'). Start a goal-setting conversation with a background statement to give employees context. Explain as much of the *why* as you possibly can. This will assist employees in making the best decisions as new things arise. Talk about how each individual's goals fit into and support the overall organization and/or team.

Key Operating Practice: Provide context.

If there are known challenges to achieving goals, try to describe the positive aspects of things as well as what might get in the way. Relate the goals to the employees' situations or experiences so that they can develop a perspective that enables them to stay focused and aligned in their behaviors. When you disagree with the goals your team has, have the conversation with your manager, but not with the team. This is a dangerous area, and one where you have to make a tough decision: as a leader or manager in the organization, you have to work toward the company's goals or leave the organization. Acting like a victim by blaming them for the goals is not an effective or productive approach for anyone.

Effective communications is a big part of a leader's and manager's role, even when you are not discussing goals. Here are a few additional tips on how to be a great communicator:

Watch your body language

Keep your body open. Make eye contact. Show you're tuned in when you ask for information or stories from others. Lean toward the speaker. Acknowledge points with an "I see," an "uh-huh," or a nod.

Ask, restate, and respond

Ask clarifying questions. Then restate what you've heard to make sure you've got it right. ("So you're saying that....") Ask probing questions when you sense anger, frustration, or disagreement. Restate what the other person is saying by capturing the essence, but leaving out any volatile phrases or language. Check your understanding. Summarize facts and feelings. Respond to show you are listening in good faith. Possible responses include simply stating that you sympathize or appreciate the communication, or stating that you will take no action for a certain reason. Make your response clear and, if you indicate you will take further action, do so.

Defuse

Show empathy with the speaker, even if you don't agree with his or her point ("You sound worried, Bill."). Reframe issues. Focus on the interests, not positions. Try to always use "I" language instead of "You." Rather than saying, "When you do that, you make me feel..." say, "When you do that, I feel...."

Listen

Stop talking—to others and to yourself. Listen between the lines for implicit meanings as well as explicitly stated ones. Instead of accepting a person's remarks as the whole story, look for omissions—things left unsaid or unexplained—which should logically be present. Notice the speaker's nonverbal communication. Is he or she enthusiastic, angry, or nervous? What is the intent of the speaker's communication? Speak affirmatively while listening. Confine yourself to constructive replies until the context has shifted, and criticism can be offered without blame.

Chapter 2 Executables

➤ Communicating the strategic framework is an ongoing process.

➤ Link individual and team goal-setting to the strategic framework to provide context.

➤ Inform employees and teams.

    ❧ Plan your communications so they will be effective.

    ❧ Divulge comprehensive information (as much as possible within all applicable laws and regulations, and considering the competitive environment).

    ❧ Prepare and structure your initial presentations.

        ➤ Share why the organization exists.

        ➤ Discuss behaviors/values/operating principles in terms of what excellence looks like.

- ➤ Present where the company is going.
- ➤ Note the areas of focus/strategies for the whole organization.
    - • Present the *what* and the *how*.
    - • Share timelines and details.

➤ Keep the following in mind when you inform.

- ❧ Think through multiple perspectives.
- ❧ Talk about what the destination and other elements of the strategic planning framework mean to you as a leader/manager.
- ❧ Identify things that will not be changing.

➤ Provide written follow-up to all employees on an ongoing basis.

➤ Seek explicit commitment from people throughout the organization.

➤ Conduct individual goal-setting.

➤ Inspire employees on an ongoing basis.

- ❧ Discuss the aspirational components of your strategic framework on an ongoing basis.

➤ Engage the organization in reaching the destination.

- ❧ Share stories of success and challenges.
- ❧ Measure your progress.

➤ Role-model that goal-setting is critical to the organization's success.

➤ Manage the change necessary due to your plans or as they arise.

➤ Become a great communicator.

- ❖ Be honest as both a giver and receiver of information.
- ❖ Be attentive.
- ❖ Be polite.
- ❖ Be clear.
- ❖ Be curious.
- ❖ Provide context.

Chapter 3

Creating the Context for Excellence: Developing a High-Performance Culture

> *"I don't care how much you know until I know how much you care."*
>
> —Employees everywhere

Think back to a time when you did not have the tools to do your job, or when you did not feel supported in getting done what you thought had to be done, or even when you had a boss who was more of a hindrance than a help. You probably did not perform as well as you could have. Now contrast that memory with one of feeling particularly successful. How many things

> "Excellence happens in context."
>
> —The Human Factor, Inc.

or people can you list that influenced the difference in your performance? High performance and success are not dependent on one simple factor or results of one or two things. The entire context you operate in greatly affects your results. This context includes the culture of the company—how things get done, how decisions get made, what works and does not work as far as behaviors, and what gets rewarded and how—the complete environment in which employees interact with each other and with other stakeholders.

Creating clear strategic plans based on the framework explored in Chapter 1, coupled with communicating constantly and consistently to maintain clarity, helps you create the context for excellence to happen in your organization. It assists you in making the critical decisions about what is okay and what is not okay as far as both the *what* and the *how* you achieve results. It influences what systems you put in place to monitor progress, check for quality, continuously gather data, and achieve customer and employee loyalty. From clearly establishing why you exist to determining how you will behave, to creating a clear vision on where you are going, to focusing energies on the most critical few, the emphasis you put on the components of your strategic-planning framework speaks volumes and drives your culture. When you are serious about getting to your destination, it energizes you to make the changes that must be made to long-standing processes that no longer serve you well.

Build and Maintain It: Enabling Excellence

Some aspects of your culture are visible—dressing casually, demonstrating friendliness to one another, speaking up with ideas or opinions, and focusing on customers are aspects of cultures that are easy to observe. Others are more difficult to see because they represent the more subtle norms, including individual assumptions, values, and beliefs about the organization, its competitors, the customers, and other stakeholders. These aspects of the culture are often an unconscious set of forces that determine both individual and collective behaviors. Examples of this less-visible level of culture might be a belief in the importance of doing things right the first time (or you will be fired), being honest and ethical in all transactions, feeling like a part of the team and valuing collaboration, or going beyond expectations to satisfy the customer.

Elements of your culture are also visible in your mission statement and how obvious it is. There are clues to culture everywhere. How much energy is there when you walk into the lobby? Are employees talking to each other in the hallways? Are meetings run effectively or haphazard, on time or always starting late? How much time do senior executives spend with customers or otherwise out in the market? How many employee-generated ideas are implemented or even considered?

Culture helps people know what to do and how to act. Remember that actions speak much louder than words, so it is the apparent behaviors that get translated into beliefs and drive behavior throughout the organization. An aligned and positive culture can contribute significantly to an organization's success. The behaviors of everyone can contribute to getting you to your destination points. An unaligned (usually unintentionally developed) culture gets in the way and slows you down.

Cultures poorly aligned to the elements of the strategic framework can be damaging and distracting. For instance, when a company needs all employees to become obsessive about customers due to increased competition or ever-higher customer expectations, the culture has to support the employee behaviors necessary to achieve this obsession. This includes building policies and practices that allow employees to make decisions and take risks about satisfying customer requests immediately. For example, if a customer service agent is only allowed to operate "by the book" in addressing customer requests, she risks losing a customer when there is a unique need and it requires three levels of approvals to have that need met.

I recently made a mistake on a Web order. I called into the customer service department of the company I used. The mistake was my fault and, if the agent had been restricted to behaving according to a strict set of rules, it would have been tough luck for me in getting the order changed or, at the very least, there would have been additional charges. Instead, the customer service agent empathized with me and used a "se-cret" code to change my order without an additional cost or hassle on my part. She was empowered to make it right for me because the company is customer-obsessive and builds in the flexibility to operate that way at all levels.

Now imagine if I had called that same company and the emphasis was on operating efficiency, standards, and policies versus being customer-obsessive. The agent might have said, "I'm sorry, but you made a mistake and there is nothing we can do." Or she might have changed my order to make it cor-rect, but charged me. After all, the mistake was clearly mine. But she did not do either of these things. She used her judg-ment and made it right because she knows that a critical com-ponent of the company's success is in retaining customers and because she is clear that being customer obsessed is one very powerful way to do that. She is empowered to make daily, even minute-by-minute decisions that contribute to the company's success.

Every company has a culture. The key to building a high-performing culture is to make sure you consider *what* and *how* you will get to your destination points. Work to imagine what the norms in the organization need to be to enable everyone to work effectively on the right initiatives. For instance, if you were trying to be more innovative to enable new product de-velopment or new services, what would a great meeting dis-cussion on new product concepts look like? What would you hear people saying? What would you see employees doing be-fore the meeting to prepare, during the meeting to engage, and after the meeting to act?

Now consider what you would see if you looked today? How much change is required? How can you clarify and re-ward the behaviors you desire and enact appropriate conse-quences for undesirable behavior? What elements of the culture need to change? Are there beliefs getting in the way? Are there rewards that encourage things to stay the same?

Any changes you feel necessary should be mapped within your breakthrough model and considered part of your strategy for moving forward. And remember that leadership and management behaviors (not words) are the single greatest influence on an organization's culture.

Leaving culture changes to chance is like abandoning one-half of your strategic-planning framework. It is like pretending that those darn employees and the way they get things done do not really matter to achieving success.

Cultures are difficult to change, and it takes a concerted, visible, and powerful energy to shift them. One of the real benefits to completing your strategic framework and communicating it constantly is that it will drive a culture that fully supports getting you to where you want to go. When things are clear and simple to employees, they develop a sense of direction and focus, and can move quickly. This raises the level of satisfaction with most employees today because speed can be exhilarating as long as everyone is aligned. Almost all employees want to be a part of a compelling future, want to know what is most important at work and what excellence looks like. It is not so much fun if you are going fast in a game of bumper cars, getting banged around a lot, and getting nowhere (except perhaps when you are at an amusement park for the afternoon).

When you create a culture of performance and success, you inspire loyalty with employees and other stakeholders. Who doesn't want to be part of a winning team? You also create advocates who promote the company positively to others. This energy and enthusiasm creates a virtuous cycle—the more clarity you have, the more you self-select in or out, the more you make the best decisions, the more successful you feel, the more you are surrounded by others who are focused and aligned, the more you accomplish, the more fun it is, the more you want to go the extra mile and do the right thing, the more success you and everyone in the company has!

The specifics of a high-performance culture are unique to your company because they are based on what will work best for you to get you to where you want to go within the parameters you have defined. As was mentioned in previous chapters, every decision you make, almost every behavior you engage in, has advantages and disadvantages, so there is no one perfect way. There is no one size fits all when it comes to culture.

> **Key Operating Practice:** Clearly define what winning looks like.

However, there is ample research to help us understand some commonalities for what makes a high-performing culture. Bain & Company recently released research published in *Leader to Leader* ("Culture as Competitive Advantage," Winter 2006) that outlines a shared set of practices and beliefs driving high-performance cultures. They found six attributes common across 200 high-performing companies.

The most important factor consistent for all high-performing organizations is to have clarity on what winning looks like. Completing your destination modeling is crucial to achieve this. Looking across the entire organization and defining what it looks like from a variety of perspectives helps employees relate to the vision of success.

> **Key Operating Practice:** Measure what matters and what employees can relate to.

Many strategic-planning processes focus on financial metrics solely. The problem with this is that most employees do not feel directly connected to these metrics.

They do not see how making a decision about how to handle a customer leads to achieving a desired profit margin. Oftentimes the employees rarely see the financials anyway, and when they do it is usually quarterly and annually, too far away to make the connections between their decisions and the financials. But when individuals can clearly see what it looks like when the company gets to where it is going in ways they can relate to, employees can make good decisions about their individual behavior. For example, the company I placed my Web order with is very clear with all employees that retaining customers is critical. A metric about it is included in their destination points. They have created and consistently communicate specific examples of behaviors—both what is desired and what is out of bounds. Their reward system is set up to recognize employees who exceed customer expectations. They provide training to all employees on how to live in a customer-obsessive way at work. They communicate their progress company-wide on a monthly basis. They have clearly defined what excellence looks like when they achieve success in this area.

> **Key Operating Practice:** Develop an ownership mentality and enable educated risk-taking.

This clarity enables employees to act like owners of the business. It sets the stage for individuals to make decisions in the best interest of the entire organization. *Thinking and acting like an owner at every level of the organization* is another characteristic of high-performing cultures. In addition, clarity and focus enable employees to take appropriate risks in all of their decisions. When individuals understand the boundaries in which they can operate as well as where the company wants to go, they feel empowered with a freedom to decide and act, and most often make the right choices.

High-performing organizations complement their drive to create a culture aligned to their destination points with an ongoing vigilance of looking at the external environment. They are constantly engaged in research and exploration about what is going on with customers, competitors, suppliers, and others. They are good at seeking and considering data-based information to refine their destination points, strategies, and initiatives. They do not rely solely on anecdotal

> **Key Operating Practice:** Keep an eye on the external environment.

evidence. As the world moves at an ever-increasing pace, monitoring the environment consistently and responding adequately will increase in importance.

The final two secrets of high-performing organizations: (1) they commit to setting up employees for success, and (2) they nurture an atmosphere of trust. This is demonstrated by giving employees the tools they need, including the training, coaching, and feedback to achieve great things, as well as engaging employees in sharing ideas and candidly discussing issues. (See more about doing these well in Chapter 4.) Constantly communicate the strategic-planning framework, including barriers and challenges to progress. (Use Chapter 2 as a checklist for doing this well.)

> **Key Operating Practice:** Set up people to succeed and nurture trust.

Numerous studies note that high-performance organizations don't take culture for granted; they plan it, monitor it, and manage it so that it remains aligned with what they want to achieve. Through the process of clearly defining your destination points, as well as creating your breakthrough model and operations plans, you will have explored both the *what* and the *how* you will get the results you want. Completing and effectively communicating your strategic framework helps drive important components of the culture. When the destination is clear, people develop a sense of direction and focus, and this in turn contributes to a thriving culture. Employees become more confident, more willing to take risks, and act quickly because they understand their impact on the big picture and overall results. Employees feel empowered when they understand the boundaries that they are expected to operate within. Those who do not feel comfortable or confident within the defined boundaries find it easier to self-select out. It becomes a virtuous cycle when the strategic framework is clear, the culture is intentionally defined, and individuals are held accountable to achieving the behaviors and results outlined in both. Higher results are a possible and, in fact, a probable, outcome.

Consider the System: Produce More of What You Need

Organizational systems and processes

So how do managers and leaders hold themselves and others accountable for staying on track and creating a context for excellence? Getting data about what is going on in your organization, especially those things that do not promote reaching your destination points, is an important part of every manager's and leader's role. This process of gathering information and returning it to the system so that behaviors can be modified or encouraged based on findings is known as organizational feedback. Organizational feedback is similar to individual feedback, but it is often provided broadly and has a more far-reaching impact.

Feedback, done organizationally via meetings and company-wide communications as well as individually (as explored fully in Chapter 4), is critical for building a self-reinforcing system. Talent development committees (succession planning), staffing, promotion, communications, and performance management are all systems or processes that include elements of organizational and individual feedback.

Superior performance is the combination of the systems and processes as well as many different conditions working together to create the right set of outputs. Poor performance can often be created by the misalignment of a few of these qualities and conditions. Some of the most common system factors that contribute to individual employee performance are:

External Factors:
➤ **Equipment and Resources.**

Access to the appropriate tools, money, people, and so on required to do the tasks.

➤ **Job Content and Logistics.**

Availability of the appropriate information required for the job. Timelines and appropriate coordination that support achieving results.

➤ **Personality/Style and Culture.**

The degree to which there is alignment between the way the individual goes about communicating and performing the tasks related to the job, and the organization's expectations for how they are done.

Internal Factors:
➤ **Clarity and Understanding.**

The degree to which the individual truly understands what is expected and how he or she is expected to get it done.

➤ **Skill Set.**

Having the right set of competencies, skills, and knowledge required for the job.

➤ **Motivation.**

Having the internal desire and drive to complete the task.

The individual, leaders, managers, and the organization all have accountability for creating a high-performing culture. However, it is the leader or manager who must constantly act as the liaison between employees and the organization to ensure the organizational capabilities are in place to support individual performance.

In order to build a strong system of organizational feedback, you must first understand your current state. As noted in Chapter 1, focus on those areas that align with the categories you choose for destination planning. Look for data to develop your opinions. If you included addressing the gaps between your current and desired states through building a breakthrough model, you have already planned out some elements of providing organizational feedback. Review all the systems and processes you currently have in your company. Which ones recognize, reward, and perpetuate the behaviors you believe are necessary to get you to where you want to go? Are there any that are supporting behaviors that no longer serve the organization well?

Examine the following processes of the employee life cycle in your organization:

- ❥ Staffing.
- ❥ Assimilation.
- ❥ Performance management.
- ❥ Development.
- ❥ Promotion.
- ❥ Termination.

Carefully consider whether the processes you use (formal or informal) are going to help you get to your destination points or hinder the organization. A simple approach for gathering this data is to ask employees. Some example questions to examine your staffing process include:

- ❥ What do you think is most important in our hiring process?
- ❥ What are the two key messages you walked away with when you went through our recruiting process?
- ❥ What do you think we should be stressing when we recruit? (You will hear about gaps between desired state and current state in answers to this question.)
- ❥ What is one thing you would change if you were in charge of recruiting for our company?

If you do not have processes in place for these basic phases of an employee's life with your organization, you are sending some loud messages today. It is highly unlikely your lack of attention to this is serving you or the company well. When employees see a leader or manager focusing all his or her energy on financial metrics, quality metrics, or even on simple tasks, it is easy for them to create great stories about the lack of visible energy on the company's "greatest asset"! There is no quicker way to derail getting to your desired destination than to ignore the very things that attract most employees and keep them energized and aligned.

Every time you communicate with the organization or teams, even when you are *just* gathering data, you send messages about what is acceptable and what is not. More importantly, you send messages through your own behavior every day. If you have never or rarely asked for employee feedback, the first time you ask these questions, the employees' thought bubbles will likely include:

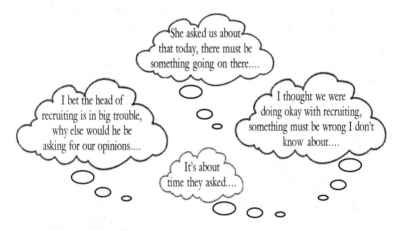

Only over time, when employees come to trust *why* you are gathering information and see *how* you actually use it, will their bubbles begin to shift. Eventually employees may come to you and offer important data. When employees go to leaders and managers with unsolicited information, ideas, or even opinions about the organization, that is when you can feel fairly comfortable you have a trust-filled organization.

Once you have developed a decent understanding of your current state, you have to create breakthrough models and/ or operational plans that clearly address how your culture will be a key part of getting to your destination. Let's face it; this is the stuff most employees are talking about in the break rooms. This is what employees really care about. How many times have you ever overheard a hallway conversation about how exciting it was to reach a certain gross profit margin or raising prices on a top-selling product? It is much more likely you are going to hear about how the company does not care about employees; after all, they just cut X or did Y....

To build a high-performing organization, you have to conduct a thorough strategic-planning process and then follow through and implement those things that are real to employees in big and small ways every day.

➤ Develop management practices that get incorporated into the way you do things all the time.

   ❧ First communicate what excellence looks like for the particular practice.

   ❧ You then have to build the skill level to do whatever it is you want.

   ❧ Provide the tools and training to teach people how to do it well.

   ❧ Follow up and demonstrate that you expect it to happen and it will remain important.

   ❧ Ask about it. Measure it.

   ❧ If it does not happen, you have to be prepared to provide immediate realigning feedback (see Chapter 4 for more details on how to do this well) and exercise consequences if you cannot modify the behavior after several tries.

➤ Teach everyone in the company how to present ideas in a positive way.

Provide a simple tool or structure and use it yourself!

➤ Teach managers how to communicate well, especially the elements of the strategic planning framework. (Refer back to Chapter 2 for tips on becoming a great communicator.)

➤ Conduct upward feedback for all senior managers and leaders in the organization.

Implement a 360° process so that managers and leaders get anonymous, direct feedback on their own behaviors. I often conduct feedback processes with senior leaders before any other work is initiated. They can be a powerful lens into current behaviors, beliefs, and ways of working. When a leadership team wants to implement 360° feedback on managers without first going through it themselves, I walk away. Doing unto others without having insight on yourself is a bad omen for what else is to come in the organization, and a red flag for me. Another principle to keep in mind when first conducting 360° feedback on leaders and managers is to make the first one a "freebie." In other words, design guiding principles about the process that include only the person being evaluated gets to see the feedback the first time. They can choose to share it with their manager, but they don't have to. This makes the process a little more comfortable for the first go-round. It presents the process as one of being helpful versus embarrassing, uncomfortable, and miserable. Giving a leader or manager candid and direct feedback is such a rare occurrence today that many people need to get it in the safest environment possible from the start. The second time 360° feedback is gathered on a manager or leader (generally six to 12 months later), the report is provided to both the individual evaluated and his or her manager.

To design a 360° process for your organization, link the desired behaviors to your strategic-planning framework. Not one set of behaviors works in every environment. You need to assess and provide feedback on what is desired, what is okay, and what is not okay **in your context**.

➤ Another option to get upward feedback is to conduct *start, stop, continue* sessions.

Someone outside the team leads these sessions. If possible, use an outside facilitator so that it is clear there are no hidden agendas. With the manager outside the room, the direct reports discuss what they want the manager to *continue doing*. What things does he or she do now that you value and find helpful in enabling your performance? What is working and what do you want him or her to continue? The direct reports then discuss what they want the manager to *stop doing*. What is getting in the way of performance excellence? The group wraps up with what they want the manager to *start doing*. What new, very specific behaviors do they need the manager to start doing so that they can individually and as a team be their best? All of these behavioral changes are documented, and the manager then returns to the room. The facilitator presents the list to the manager and allows him or her a few minutes to digest the input. The manager then must commit to what he or she feels can be committed to as far as behavioral change. This becomes a contract with the team, and is written down and shared with the team. It is not just one-way at this point, however. Employees must commit that they will provide feedback to the manager and support him or her in behaving in new ways. This might be encouraging the manager when he or she continues something that is working well. It might mean reminding the manager, privately, of a commitment to stop doing something or to ask the manager for something that is desired and on the start list. A *start, stop, continue* process can take as little as an hour to conduct and usually has a fairly dramatic impact on shifting behaviors. It is important that it is a two-way process. It is not about setting a manager up to be criticized, hurt, or demeaned in any way. It is about becoming clear on what excellence looks like to enable an entire team to move toward its destination points.

➤ Expect ongoing, effective one-on-one conversations between all people, managers, and their direct reports.

Provide tools and templates for the types of things managers should talk about on a continuing basis. Do not assume managers and leaders or employees know how to participate in effective one-on-one conversations. There is a reason they are not happening today in your organization. I often hear that there simply is not enough time. But that is really an excuse that does not hold up to scrutiny. After all, what is more important than understanding what motivates your employees, finding ways you can help them produce more, understanding what is getting in the way of their success, keeping them aligned and focused on the goals, gaining a better understanding of what is going on in your team...? I have yet to meet a manager who could answer this one in a way that would let him or her off the hook from scheduling and conducting regular one-on-one meetings. I have heard some creative and even sad excuses, but the bottom line is that, if you do a good job communicating regularly with your direct reports, it will save you countless hours of time in rework, in resetting expectations, and in redoing what someone else was sure was right.

> Remember that the mantra "there is never time to do it right, but always time to do it over" does not really apply in high-performing organizations.

There are probably a hundred great questions managers and leaders can use in regularly scheduled one-on-one meetings. I have noted some of my favorites for you here. Once you do these for a few months, you will find there are questions that work well for you.

➤ What is new since we last met?

➤ Tell me something you are proud of that you've accomplished since our last meeting. What are you feeling good about?

➤ What has surprised you (something that was harder than you thought it would be or easier than you thought it would be)?

➤ What do you wish you had more time to do?

➤ What do you think is most critical to make happen in the next three months?

➤ Are there any important decisions you are facing? What else do you need to be able to make them?

➤ How can I best support you?

➤ Are there tools or resources, including people I can introduce you to, that I might be able to get for you?

➤ Is there anything you think you should stop doing? If you did, what impact would that have?

➤ If you were hired to consult with our company, what would you do?

➤ What is a process or activity that, if you made an improvement, would give you and others the greatest return on time, energy, and dollars invested?

➤ What is the most important thing you and I should be talking about? Describe the issue to me.

　❧ How is this currently affecting you?

　❧ Who or what else is being affected?

- ❧ If nothing changes, what are the implications?

- ❧ What's the most important first step you can take to begin to resolve this issue?

- ❧ What do you need from me to support you in doing this?

- ❧ What exactly are you committed to do and by when?

- ❧ When and how should I follow up with you?

➤ What is currently impossible to do that, if it were possible, would change everything?

➤ What area within your responsibility are you most satisfied with? The least satisfied with? What would you most like to change about your job?

➤ Who on your team are your strongest employees? What are you doing to make sure they are happy and motivated?

➤ Who are your weakest employees? What are you doing to give them the feedback and support they need to modify their behavior and results?

➤ What topic are you hoping I won't bring up?

Most employees have never had these types of meetings, so ease into them in your organization. Schedule one-on-one meetings on a monthly basis or whatever time frame works best for you; however, it does need to happen at least every other month to have any kind of impact. Scheduling them and cancelling them or constantly postponing them does not count. Remember the messages you will send and the bubbles you create when you do not stick to your own or the organization's commitments!

In a high-performing organization, structured conversations between managers and direct reports are common and occur on a regular basis. They are not unusual events, striking fear in the hearts of an employee as soon as the meeting shows up on the calendar.

Another effective concept that was introduced in recent years is feed forward. The term *feed forward* was coined in conversations between Jon Katzenbach, author of *The Wisdom of Teams* and *Peak Performance*, and Marshall Goldsmith, executive coach and author of *What Got You Here Won't Get You There*. Feed forward is a complement to feedback (which will be presented in detail in Chapter 4). It is based on the premise that you can provide suggestions for the future and help people get to where they want to go without bringing up the negative actions from their pasts. Feed forward can be a more expansive and positive experience for individuals, managers, and leaders. As part of ongoing one-on-one conversations, managers and leaders can incorporate this notion of future focus through the following steps:

- Ask the employee about one behavior he or she would like to change.

- Provide two suggestions for performing the behavior well in the future.

- Thank the employee for listening to the suggestions and move on.

This approach leaves the receiver of the information in a position of thanks. The employee has received a gift that is not tied to any negative behavior from his or her past, and he or she is more likely to want to receive additional suggestions in the future. Feed forward can be a powerful developmental tool especially because it provides another mechanism for you to define excellence in line with your strategic-planning framework. Feed forward is a process that works well when a whole team is involved. Individuals note a behavior they want to change. Participants then pair up in the room and one member of the pair describes the behavior (for example, "I want to be better organized."). The pair then has one minute to provide ideas for ways to perform the behavior well in the future.

There is no discussion of the past. The partners switch, and, after another minute, thank each other and pair up with another team member. Consider pairing people with partners they do not work with on a consistent and regular basis. This will help eliminate any judgments of past behavior when offering suggestions.

Be prepared for a real increase in energy in the room when you do this exercise with a team. After the first two minutes, you will find participants loud and excited about getting helpful advice in such a positive manner. Successful individuals enjoy getting ideas that are intended to support them in achieving their goals. In addition, people tend to listen more attentively when getting helpful advice about the future versus judgments about their individual behaviors from the past. Incorporating feed forward into your ongoing conversations and occasionally in team meetings supports building a high-performing culture. It does take practice and needs to be considered an important management exercise to stay on your to-do list.

Before you embark on some of these management practices, you should assess the managers' and leaders' effectiveness in conducting and participating in these types of conversations. Do not assume your managers are naturally good at it, and do not assume employees are ready to participate effectively, either. Remember, your system produces exactly what it is set up to produce, so there are many reasons you do not currently practice feed forward. After years of reading 360° surveys and organizational assessments, I have observed that it is fairly consistent that managers and leaders have ample room for improvement in one-on-one conversations with direct reports. Direct reports have some deeply ingrained beliefs and bubbles that have to be shifted as well. After all, if none of these things has ever happened, it is a significant change to incorporate them into *the way things are done here*.

Manage Performance: Give Me What I Need to Be Successful

Performance management is a powerful process to complement your strategic planning framework. Unfortunately, when performance management is mentioned, most leaders, managers, and employees cringe. Lengthy forms and bureaucratic processes come immediately to mind. Effective performance management, however, drives what gets measured (or doesn't), how linked individuals are to the company and team goals (or not), and what gets rewarded (or ignored), and therefore perpetuated in your organization.

According to recent research, 78 percent of all company leaders note "getting the right things done" as a significant problem in their companies. Accountability has become a critical competency missing in many companies. How many of us have ever gone into a meeting where people promised deliverables and then nothing ever materialized? How many of us have ever committed to a deadline only to see it come and go, all the while holding our breaths that no one would notice? Or worse, we were the only ones who completed our portion of the work just to watch others "get away" with not doing theirs? Is there a lot of public commitment, but employees go back to doing what is on their own agendas as soon as the meeting is over? This is another area where speed does not necessarily serve us well today. We are running so fast, and almost everyone has too many demands on their time. We don't find the time to do the things we commit to and feel are important to do. We only have enough time to react to the crisis of the day or respond to a seemingly urgent issue.

After your initial communication regarding your strategic planning framework, your performance-management process can enable ongoing efforts to build accountability, and keep everyone and everything in the organization focused and aligned. Unfortunately, without a strong performance-management system in place, most of us get off track easily and forget to measure what we have told everyone is important.

There are many benefits to approaching performance management as an ongoing practice and incorporating it into other management practices versus an annual event. An effective performance management system:

- ❧ Communicates how individuals contribute to business success and how they will be evaluated.

- ❧ Aligns individual goals with key business priorities, resulting in greater focus, better use of resources, and reduced non-value-added activity.

- ❧ Provides a comprehensive system for recognizing *what* gets done and reinforcing *how* it is achieved.

- ❧ Creates a discipline of measuring progress against specific goals and making adjustments as necessary.

- ❧ The Performance Management Cycle involves five steps that are represented by the graphic.

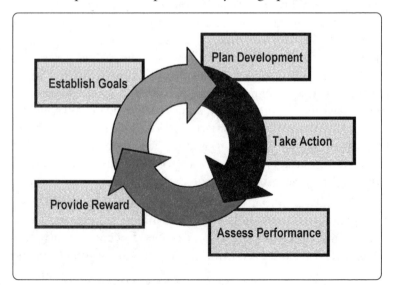

The circular arrows represent the general sequence that the steps follow and suggest the continuous nature of the process. Although they are shown sequentially, in reality, leaders and managers must move between the steps somewhat freely. The five steps are:

1. Establish Goals

   Link what needs to get done to the strategic planning framework and align the competencies, skills, and knowledge of the associate to create specific action items that will be the employee's focus moving forward.

2. Plan Development

   Discuss both short- and long-term development needs, including agreement on how and when development will occur as well as prioritization of development to support more immediate business needs. A plan should be created to accomplish the learning and growth required and desired.

3. Take Action

   Provide ongoing and frequent direction and support while the employee applies energy and focus toward accomplishing the goals.

4. Assess Performance

   Evaluate the progress being made toward the goals, and provide ongoing, quality feedback to the employee both informally and formally.

5. Provide Reward

   Acknowledge and reward employees through organizational programs, local recognition, and individual employee-tailored approaches. This may also involve consequences and disciplinary action for poor performance.

The consequences of a poorly structured and implemented performance-management process are significant. Inconsistent evaluation criteria and rewards unmatched to actual performance can lead to mistrust, lower productivity, and higher attrition. If top performers see no difference in how they are rated and what opportunities they have, morale suffers. Lack of documentation, visibility, and accountability can negatively affect external stakeholders who are demanding more and more transparency these days.

Leaders, managers, and employees all have a role to play in creating performance excellence and supporting it through performance-management practices.

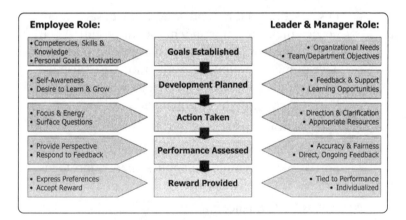

Regular, quality communication is a cornerstone to effective performance management. The criteria for quality in these conversations is to be direct; focus on both short- and longer-range goals to tie the employee's efforts and results to the overall strategic planning framework for the company; and share responsibility for making sure the employee knows what is expected, how to get it done (from a behavioral level), and when it needs to be done.

Effective performance management involves assessments that range from quick and informal "pats on the back" in the hallway to structured performance appraisals. The following is a typical annual performance management timeline.

In theory, beginning of the fiscal year	Set performance goals. In actuality, many companies never really get around to this and employees end up establishing their performance goals at year-end, just in time for annual salary adjustments. It is, after all, fairly easy to set goals after the fact!
Mid-year	Fill out a form on what the employee is doing compared to the goals if they were ever set. They are almost always focused exclusively on the *what* and can be fraught with surprises if no feedback has occurred.
Year-end	**Leader or Manager role** Conduct the obligatory year-end performance review so the form can be submitted for salary adjustments.
	Employee self-assessment The employee completes a form and submits it to his or her manager who either argues with everything in it, ignores it entirely in the process of evaluation, or uses it exclusively to make a decision.

The big difference between having a performance-management process and creating a culture of performance excellence is that many of these activities are ongoing and directly linked to the business strategies, including any changes throughout the year. The forms are unimportant. The annual review is simply a quick summary of what you and the employee already know with a final rating added. Even the best annual performance review is highly unlikely to improve performance. It is the ongoing, direct, and candid feedback discussed in detail later in this chapter coupled with an obvious link to the company's strategic planning framework that will make a difference in performance.

Formal Performance Review Discussions

The majority of this section focuses on periodic performance reviews and formal performance appraisals. However, most of the principles can be applied to any level of performance assessment situation. A properly constructed annual performance appraisal should represent a summary of ongoing, year-round dialogue.

Unfortunately, performance feedback discussions are often avoided because they may involve giving and receiving negative messages. Tough communication situations often make people feel uncomfortable. These situations challenge the best communication skills of everyone involved. In addition, we often question our own conclusions about an employee when there are performance problems. We look for reasons the employee is underperforming that are outside our control (for example, changes in structure, project scope, upper management, and client base), thus we can rationalize not addressing them. However, it is crucial that employees understand their performance levels in order to improve, maintain, and/or surpass their present levels.

Structured performance conversations should happen at least three times a year. These are in addition to the regularly scheduled one-on-one conversations you have with employees. The first session should happen at the beginning of your fiscal year and include discussions about the strategic planning framework, team or division goals, and what the expectations are for the employee for the coming year. A second formal performance management conversation should happen mid-year. This is a documented check-in session to look at progress, barriers and discuss any issues of significance as far as individual performance. At year-end, you should have a session where the employee provides a self-assessment and you discuss an overall evaluation of the year.

Prepping for formal discussions

Preparation is an essential step in clearly communicating performance feedback to an employee. The degree of thoroughness may vary based on the type of performance discussion. However, the following activities should be considered in advance of all formal discussions.

➤ Review documented performance goals.

Priorities may have shifted since those goals were written. Consider any changes and new priorities to determine what objectives the employee should be measured against.

➤ Collect performance information from various sources. Consider:

- ❧ Personal documentation of positive and negative performance.

- ❧ Others connected to the employee's work (for example, internal customers and colleagues).

- ❧ Evaluate results.

- ❧ Ask the employee to contribute his or her perceptions of performance.

➤ Create an initial assessment of performance based on the information you have available. "Initial" implies that there may be information pertinent to the evaluation that you do not currently have. This information should be discovered in a performance discussion by asking behavioral-based questions and through having the employee do a self-assessment before your meeting.

➤ Frame performance feedback points based on the initial assessment. Include specific examples to support the points. Generally, feedback provided in a formal discussion should include both strengths and areas of improvement.

Steps for planning formal performance feedback discussions

The following is a suggested planning sequence you can use as a leader or manager to help you organize your thoughts and actions for formal performance feedback discussions.

Step 1. Set up the discussion.	► Determine a date and an adequate amount of time for the discussion. ► Agree on the issues that will be discussed.
Step 2. Prepare.	► Complete your discussion planning worksheets. (See Chapter 4.) ► Examine major conclusions for any personal biases that may be affecting your observations. ► Identify the three or four key messages you want to deliver or issues you want to discuss. Write them down. ► Be ready to support all messages with examples and long-term consequences.

Step 3. Participate in the discussion.	► Assure that your time will be uninterrupted and the setting will be suitable for a candid discussion.
	 ► Establish ground rules:
	   • What you want to discuss.
	   • The importance of sharing information and conclusions candidly and openly.
	   • Your belief that both of you must work together to make the discussion work.

	➤ For each part of the discussion, ask the other person to describe his or her observations and conclusions.
Step 4. Prepare final documentation.	➤ Develop a brief written summary of the *key* points you have discussed and the actions that each person has agreed to take.
	➤ If you are documenting a performance problem, be sure to follow any additional guidelines that meet your company, state, and local regulations.

Remember that the quality of the communication between you and the other person is the key to success. Forms and worksheets can be aids, but not ends in and of themselves. Use these materials as thinking, planning, and discussion aids to support excellence in your formal performance discussions.

Performance feedback discussions are comprised of three qualities: **content**, **intent**, and **extent**.

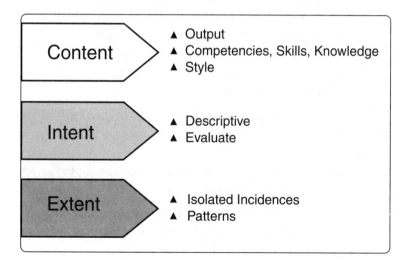

Being aware of these qualities can help you plan for your discussions.

The content of a performance feedback discussion can include three subject areas:

1. **Outputs.**

   The employee's accomplishments. What he or she produces.

2. **Competencies, Skills, and Knowledge.**

   The employee's abilities and understanding about work.

3. **Style.**

   The approach the associate takes with people, information, and events when getting things done.

The intent of a performance-feedback discussion can be descriptive or evaluative. Both of these approaches can be used to affect changed behavior.

- **Descriptive feedback** is telling someone what you've observed about his or her outputs, competencies, skills, knowledge, or style. It is most useful in supporting a person's development.

- **Evaluative feedback** is when someone's performance is judged against standards or values. It is typically used in the context of appraisal discussions.

The extent of a performance-feedback discussion can include observations about isolated incidents or patterns over time.

- **Isolated incidents** are specific behaviors and/or attitudes that are observed in a specific situation.

- **Patterns** over time are behaviors and/or attitudes that consistently affect the quality of outputs, competencies, skills, knowledge, or style.

Effective performance discussions

The actual performance discussion with an employee can be difficult for some leaders and managers. Giving feedback, especially if it involves negative information, can be an uncomfortable situation. However, the conversation is critical to ensuring that an employee has the information to be a productive contributor in the organization.

➤ The right environment.

- ❧ Establish a setting, time frame, and location that are appropriate for the discussion. Generally it should provide privacy and contribute to an open exchange of communication.

- ❧ You should not allow interruptions or try to work on other things at the same time. Privacy and your full attention are imperative to success. When you look at the phone each time it rings or check your computer screen when you get an incoming message, what are you communicating? It is difficult for an employee to take your input seriously if you really don't have the time or interest to give it appropriately.

➤ Focus.

- ❧ Come in to the meeting with the major points of feedback already in mind and documented.

- ❧ Keep the discussion centered on the data, rather than emotions or opinions.

- ❧ Avoid tangents. Bring the discussion back gently as soon as they occur.

- ❧ Focus on the desired outcome from the feedback. Do not get stuck in past behavior. Concentrate on the solution.

➤ Tone.

  ❧ Establish a tone that reflects the feedback. A light-hearted feeling may be appropriate for a congratulatory talk. However, it would be inappropriate for a serious performance problem.

  ❧ In difficult discussions, display empathy while maintaining directness and objectivity.

  ❧ Be open to hearing new information that may change your perspective.

➤ Setting.

  ❧ Select a setting that enhances discussion.

  ❧ Ensure the location is private, especially for difficult discussions.

  ❧ Minimize physical barriers (for example, desks). If in an office, move to the same side of the desk or to adjacent corners at a table.

➤ Outcomes.

  ❧ Agree on concrete outcomes. Be diligent about reaching common understanding about action items coming out of the meeting.

  ❧ Be clear on what will be done, by when, and by whom to address any problems and more fully support superior performance.

Employee Self-Assessments

By making me do a self-assessment, my boss is basically asking me to do his work for him.

Last time I did a self-assessment, my boss was supposed to complete the form before we met, instead she just commented on my remarks. What a joke!

Do these employees' thought bubbles sur- prise you? They shouldn't. They are the most common beliefs that go through employees' minds when you ask them to perform a self-assessment, usually only at year-end. Employee self-assessments can be a valuable tool if structured and used prop- erly in the performance-management process. Provide a template or structure to employees and a time frame for com- pleting their self-assessment. Leaders and managers should operate within the same time frame and complete the formal draft assessment of the employee. As was mentioned earlier with the concept of feed forward, this tool is perfect for gain- ing insight into what the employee sees as his or her strengths, and the areas in which your support can improve performance. The self-assessment is *not* meant to be the only input for the employee's performance review. It should complement leader or manager data gathered and firsthand observations.

> You really cannot be honest when you rate yourself. Rankings that are higher or lower than what your boss thinks just send the wrong messages. It's a lose-lose situation.

An employee self-assessment can be an especially valu- able means of adapting to the different generations in the workforce today. The Baby Boomers and Traditionalists are not accustomed to this type of self-reflection, and, given that they make up a majority of the leaders and managers in orga- nizations, it is not a readily used tool. They are now managing the younger Generation Xers and Millennials, who are eager to determine their value in the organization, so the Baby Boomers and Traditionalists could find the use of self-assess- ment a tremendous way of closing the generational gap when it comes to mentoring and leading. The manner and degree in which the younger employees rate themselves can be a power- ful means to assist in their professional development. When there are disconnects between an employee's self-rating and a manager or leader's perceptions, you have a solid basis for open communication on standards of excellence and expectations.

The following is a sample self-assessment.

➤ Provide a summary of your key performance objectives for the year.

➤ What were your significant accomplishments this year?

➤ What were the major difficulties in achieving your goals and why?

➤ What general comments do you have about your performance this year?

➤ What areas of your performance do you feel you could improve? Consider both *what* you do and *how* you do it.

- ❧ Knowledge of the job.
- ❧ Quality of work.
- ❧ Quantity of work.
- ❧ Dependability and accountability.
- ❧ Decision-making, problem-solving, and judgment.
- ❧ Communication skills.
- ❧ Interpersonal relationships/collaboration.
- ❧ Initiative/resourcefulness/creativity.
- ❧ Effective use of time.

➤ What are your top three developmental goals for next year? Why?

The self-assessment is generally administered as part of the year-end process. You can also incorporate it into your mid-year discussions once your culture fully embraces the concept. One thing to look for, especially once you have built a high-performing culture, is an inverse correlation between the performance of employees and their self-ratings. High performers are often very demanding of themselves and see all too clearly how far they fall short of their ideals. Lower performers sometimes narrow their views and have a hard time accurately comparing themselves to excellence because they feel they are working hard and that must mean they are doing a good job.

Use the following tool to asses *your own* abilities and beliefs in providing effective feedback and supporting an influential performance-management process.

Activities/ Behaviors	How well do you currently perform these activities?					How important is this to the company's success?				
	Critical	Very important	Important	Not so important	Does not matter	Outstanding	Pretty good	Okay, not great	Need some help	Never done it
Put aside fears and communicate what you really think and feel.										
Present concrete, candid, and timely information.										
Provide access to equipment and resources so that the team has what it needs to achieve excellence.										
Set performance objectives with my direct reports, including timelines and behavioral expectations.										
Demonstrate my belief that ongoing feedback is important to the individual, to the team, and to the company.										

Activities/ Behaviors	How important is this to the company's success?					How well do you currently perform these activities?				
	Critical	Very important	Important	Not so important	Does not matter	Outstanding	Pretty good	Okay, not great	Need some help	Never done it
Clearly communicate what excellence looks like in terms of both the *what* and the *how*.										
Provide/support training so employees can achieve their objectives.										
Follow up with employees on feedback discussed.										
Present ideas and options in a positive manner.										
Seek feedback about myself.										
Conduct regular one-on-one meetings with all of my direct reports.										
Believe our performance-management system supports our success.										
Plan development with my direct reports.										
Accurately assess employees' performances using data from a variety of sources.										

Activities/ Behaviors	How important is this to the company's success?					How well do you currently perform these activities?				
	Critical	Very important	Important	Not so important	Does not matter	Outstanding	Pretty good	Okay, not great	Need some help	Never done it
Provide rewards appropriate for the performance and the individual.										
Prepare for formal performance discussions.										
Remain open and listen to the employees' self-assessment.										
Appropriately document all performance worthy of a mention, including positive and constructive information.										
Create the right environment for healthy performance conversations.										
Consider others' needs, wants, and views.										
Communicate to achieve conscious, intentional, and specific results.										
Put aside fears and opinions and accept feedback from others.										

Chapter 3 Executables

➤ A context for excellence can be achieved with a clear strategic plan coupled with communicating constantly and consistently to maintain clarity.

➤ The key to building a high-performing culture is to make sure you consider *what* and *how* you will get to your destination points.

    ❥ Work to imagine what the norms in the organization need to be to enable everyone to work effectively on the right initiatives.

    ❥ The culture helps people know *what* to do and *how* to act. Consider what elements of your culture have been developed simply out of nonverbal cues.

➤ What are some of the assumptions that are made about your culture based on the actions of the top-level leaders as well as the frontline representatives of your organization?

    ❥ Determine the most appropriate ways to clarify and reward the behaviors you desire and enact appropriate consequences for undesirable behavior?

➤ Five core practices and beliefs driving high-performance cultures:

1. Clearly define what winning looks like.

2. Measure what matters and what employees can relate to.

3. Develop an ownership mentality and enable educated risk-taking.

4. Keep an eye on the external environment.

5. Set up people to succeed and nurture trust.

➤ Organizational feedback has far-reaching impact, and it is based on gathering information and using the data to modify or encourage behaviors based on those findings.

❧ Are you addressing the gaps between your current and desired states through building a breakthrough model?

❧ Review all the systems and processes you currently have in the company. Which ones recognize, reward, and perpetuate the behaviors you believe are necessary to get you to your destination?

➤ Effective performance management drives what gets measured, how linked individuals are to the company and team goals, and what gets rewarded, and therefore perpetuated, in your organization.

➤ Your performance-management process can enable ongoing efforts to build accountability and keep everyone and everything in the organization focused and aligned. Without a strong performance-management system in place, most of us get off track easily and forget to measure what we have told everyone is important.

➤ The performance-management cycle consists of the following phases and is ongoing:

❧ Establish goals.

❧ Plan development.

❧ Take action.

❧ Assess performance.

❧ Provide reward.

➤ Keys to an effective performance discussion:

❧ The right environment.

❧ Focus.

❧ Tone.

❧ Setting.

❧ Outcomes.

Chapter 4

Sustaining Alignment: Positive and Constructive Feedback

Tell Me: Just Give It to Me
Feedback as a critical element to high performance

As noted in Chapter 2, leader and manager recognition of employee job performance rates among the top eight most important factors determining job satisfaction. Each of us is driven in some way by receiving feedback on our performances. We are constantly looking for it, in the spoken and certainly the unspoken. High performers and the Millennial generation currently entering the workforce crave it even more than we have seen in the past. Feedback is an important part of accelerating high performance, changing behavior within a specific business context, gaining insights, and agreeing on the standards of individual performance.

Getting to the destination requires a concerted, aligned effort across the organization. As was reviewed in Chapter 1, it is critical to have everyone in the organization heading in the same direction, and operating from the same set of behavioral guidelines. Without this alignment, employees work hard, but often on the wrong things because they must make decisions based on very limited data. With so many things competing for our attention at work and all the opportunities for us to lose focus, ongoing communication, including feedback, helps keep everyone on track.

In *The One Minute Manager*, feedback was described as ongoing (and mostly one-way) conversations with employees to either praise or reprimand. Today, feedback can be much more complex, and an even more important element of a high-performing culture. As for the concept, and even terminology stemming from *reprimand*, we have come a long way.

Twenty-five years ago, formal feedback at work was rare. You might have had an annual meeting with your manager to receive notice of your salary increase. If you were lucky, you might also have received some information about how you were doing in your role, with perhaps a 1–5 rating system on a few categories. Typically, and unfortunately, employees most often received feedback in these meetings by what was not said and by how large or how small their salary increase was in relation to the expectation.

Although almost everything in our world of work has changed in the past 25 years, this is one area that has not seen a lot of progress. When interviewed, most employees still feel they only get feedback once or twice a year in a formally scheduled performance-management meeting with their boss (after the meeting has been cancelled and rescheduled numerous times).

Virtually every employee I have ever come across desires more feedback.

Today the different generations in the workforce vary greatly in expectations and behavior in this area. In general, Traditionalists are looking for public recognition, responsibility, and an acknowledgement of accomplishments—both the team's and his or hers individually. Baby Boomers also desire public recognition for a job well done and like to receive it from their manager as well as from peers. Baby Boomers have more need for control, so providing effective feedback helps them feel more in control of *what* to work on and *how*. Generation Xers are motivated more by how their actions contribute to the organization's success. Feedback on how their individual progress affects the company and its achievements is important. Generation Xers also desire ongoing recognition from their bosses because of their experience and mindset about competing in the workforce. In addition, they enjoy constant learning, so feedback can be presented in ways that offer opportunities to grow and develop. The Millennials live in a world of social networking where feedback is a part of everyday activity. For them, giving feedback is just a way of being. The frequency in which they provide it to others varies dramatically from previous generations. Unfortunately, although Millennials participate in it a lot, they are not necessarily skilled at how to provide effective feedback. Their tremendous amount of connection to others electronically does not necessarily equate to quality face-to-face interpersonal connections.

Most companies want to implement feedback throughout the organization. When you really probe to get to the underlying reasons, they typically revolve around senior management wanting feedback for themselves and/or believing it would be a good thing, but knowing they do not currently give it or receive it. I have never spoken with a business leader or manager who does not think feedback is desirable. However, the reasons for not providing it to direct reports and seeking it themselves vary dramatically. Limiting beliefs include: "That's just not the way we do things," "Isn't that what my annual review is for?" "My boss is not really into saying how he feels," "If I were doing something wrong, they would tell me," "If I asked for it, I would only hear the bad things," "My team does not like getting input," "There is just not enough time," and the generational indicator of "I never got it and I turned out fine."

The first thing to ask yourself is *What does our system or culture currently produce?* Is the company generally good at feedback, but there are pockets where it is not occurring? Have you tried to launch feedback processes in the past and they have failed? Are employees asking for feedback (via surveys, anonymous input, and so on)? Are you getting the amount and quality of feedback linking your individual performance to the business strategy? Do you yourself have a genuine belief in the value of feedback?

When you define the pieces of your strategic-planning framework, you will be making many decisions about feedback. You may call it out explicitly as one of your guiding principles or organizational attributes. Hopefully, you will have included it as a category in your destination modeling (as recommended) and, even if you do not, it is certainly incorporated into the destination points regarding work processes and metrics; tools, systems, and technologies; and your branding/ reputation. It is also implicitly driven by what you choose as your key operating achievements. If you choose exclusively financial metrics without ever touching on qualitative measures, you are sending a loud message to the organization and building a culture that is driven purely by *what* and potentially unconcerned with *how*.

Push yourself to examine what is getting in the way of feedback in your organization. Think through your current system or culture. Are leaders and managers conducting conversations?

Do team members offer their input and ideas to others? Is it okay to give advice to colleagues and your boss? Are there missed targets with employees saying, "If only they had asked..." or "We knew all along, but no one listens..."?

The following are the most common reasons employees do not engage in feedback:

- Individuals and teams cling to old ways of doing things because they were probably successful doing it that way in the past. Even with significant changes around them, employees seek the comfort of some continuity in approach, so they do not seek information that would change their habits.

- When new goals and destination points are not inspirational, it is easy to quickly forget them and rely on tried-and-true patterns of behavior.

- Old "wisdom" is passed on to new hires. Employees quickly teach others "how things are done here" so new ideas and ways of doing things are squelched.

- A low tolerance for criticism exists in many organizations because we generally do not know how to effectively provide truly constructive feedback.

- Bad past experiences with unskilled managers and leaders makes everyone hesitant to be the first one to try feedback, so it never gets any traction or becomes part of operating practices.

Before you can provide feedback, you first need to look at *what* your employees are doing and *how* they are doing it. Let's consider your workforce in its current form. Your first instinct may be to look only at *what* and *how* much the employee accomplishes, in essence, the quantifiable outcomes. Others of you may look instead at how the employee is producing the deliverables. Either way, your initial reaction is likely based on how much time and energy you are spending with certain members of your workforce. For instance, if your primary challenges are based on your assessment that you have low performers who do not produce enough (sales, product, new clients, etc.), you are probably spending a great deal of your time on the *what* of your business—training, product knowledge, and networking opportunities. If, however, you continually spend your time "putting out fires," reassigning team members, or counseling, you are more attuned to *how* your staff is getting their jobs done.

One way to better understand where to spend your time most effectively is to look at a visual representation of your workforce. Consider for a moment that each of your salespeople or customer service/account representatives falls into one of the following four quadrants with regard to overall job performance.

Values & Results Matrix

High values **Low results** Coach & develop in competencies & skills	**High values** **High results** Encourage & reward
Low values **Low results** Provide feedback & terminate if changes are not achieved immediately	**Low values** **High results** Provide feedback & coach initially; terminate if quick movement on values doesn't occur

Values (vertical axis) — Results (horizontal axis)

Both *what* an associate does and *how* he or she does it is critical to performance excellence and reaching your destination points.

High Values, High Results: These are your top performers, your gems. So how do you make sure they don't go off to the competition? If they are really good, chances are other companies are recruiting them. What makes them stay with you? Because they are all-around great employees, besides their sales numbers or company-wide recognition awards, how else are you showing or telling them how valuable they are? Sometimes the trap we fall into is to just leave them alone. We figure they know how well they do, and "they are paid accordingly; what else do they need to hear from me on a weekly or monthly basis?" We tend to spend the least amount of our time with this group. Make sure you have an active re-recruiting plan in place for employees you rate in this category.

Low Values, High Results: If an associate produces results, but does it in a manner that alienates others, costs more money, or creates additional problems, the associate must be coached on the *how* of getting things done. Many organizations have individuals who fall into this lower right-hand quadrant of the grid. These are the associates you tend to spend a lot of your time with, trying to explain why the way he or she does things is not consistent with your strategic planning framework. They are the ones who others avoid. Continuing to condone, accept, or reward them based on their level of results sends a very loud message to the other employees. Without even making a conscious effort, you are communicating to others what is acceptable behavior and even, in some cases, that results are more important than values or operating principles. These are the employees most leaders and managers spend the majority of their time with. For many reasons, when someone is producing results, we hesitate discussing with them an adjustment to *how* they are getting the results. Sometimes we are afraid the employee will leave and we will lose a strong contributor to results. When you objectively consider the investment of time and damage recovery typically involved with employees who do not behave in acceptable ways to achieve results, you will quickly see it is a losing proposition if they can not shift their *how*.

High Values, Low Results: On the other hand, if an associate seems to be a "good" person, with high integrity, and is generally likeable by others but does not produce results, that individual needs to be coached on achieving results. These are often employees who need greater clarity on *what* needs to get done, and by when. They may also need training, tools, or other resources to get done what you want done. This coaching will be time well spent. You and the employee will be able to acknowledge immediately when he or she accomplishes small wins in this area.

Low Values, Low Results: Employees in this quadrant are sometimes bullies or otherwise intimidating to leaders and managers as well as their colleagues. Perhaps they have been around a long time or have deep technical knowledge you are afraid you cannot live without. With employees in this quadrant, you must address the situation quickly and decisively. Before I state the obvious solution to this issue, ask yourself, *As his manager, what have I done to clarify expectations in both* what *and* how *with this employee? And if the* how *can be adjusted, is there a good fit somewhere else in the organization where the employee can achieve the* what? It is your responsibility to do the best you can with this low performer and then move on. Do not spend so much time in this quadrant that you neglect those who can truly benefit from your coaching and feedback.

Take a few minutes and write down the names of your employees in each of the appropriate corresponding boxes on the grid. Be careful, however, to rate them based on their overall performance and not on an individual behavior just yet.

Once you have done that, now look at the employees who you spend the most amount of time with coaching, correcting behavior, rewarding, or disciplining. On which quadrant do you spend most of your time? Be honest with yourself. Based on your own management and leadership style, the answer may seem obvious. What does that say about the effectiveness and efficiency of your organization, your team, and your day? Do you spend time with those who have High Values and High Results because it is easier and less stressful? Do you spend a great deal of time struggling with those who are Low Results and High Values because there is something tangible to work toward, something measurable you can watch for as a sign that you are a good manager? What about those staff members who you put in the two Low Values sections? What are you doing to help their progress or their departure?

If you consider the 80/20 rule, you should be spending 20 percent of your time and effort on the things (strategies, decisions, and employees) that contribute 80 percent to achieving your strategic plan. If, however, you are spending 80 percent of your time on employees who have high results and low values, it is time for a shift in focus back to what is best for the organization. If the feedback and coaching is not working, you must do what is best for the organization (and morale) overall. This is an easy one to say, but increasingly difficult to do. Short-term results have such visible value to an organization today. The usually hidden costs of dealing with employees who get results in an unacceptable manner make it hard to justify losing a "top performer."

Now that you have considered the overall performance of your employees and placed them in the corresponding boxes on the values and results matrix, dive deeper with regard to each direct report.

❧ Consider the significant responsibilities or tasks for each employee or group of employees with similar roles. For ease of the exercise, number the significant responsibility or task.

❧ Get clear on the values or operating principles for your team and for the organization as a whole.

❧ By individual, for each significant responsibility or task, rate which quadrant the performance falls into.

The following is an abbreviated example for an account executive or salesperson.

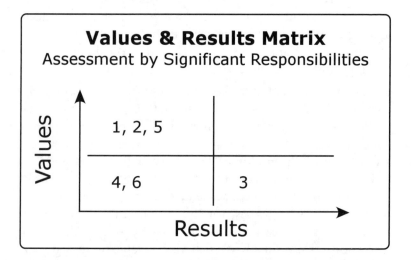

Values & Results Matrix
Assessment by Significant Responsibilities

Values

1, 2, 5

4, 6   3

Results

1. Lead generation.
2. Builds rapport with potential customers.
3. Communicates well (directly, honestly, and timely) in writing as well as verbally.
4. Negotiates to achieve win-win scenarios.
5. Follows up to deliver as promised.
6. Acquires repeat business.

Now consider why you rated the individual behaviors for the employee the way you did.

High Value, Low Results: Is the employee new to the company and/or new to the role, and has not yet had the time to produce the specific results expected? Is the employee capable of (has the right competencies, skills, and knowledge required for) this task?

High Value, High Results: Does the employee know he or she is a high performer in these responsibilities? Is he or she challenged both emotionally and intellectually to continue doing a great job in the tasks rated here? Are you leveraging his or her talents by having him or her coach others on this specific task or responsibility? Is it obvious to others the employee is a high performer in this task? How can you make it more apparent these are desired and rewarded behaviors?

The hard part for this example is that the employee has some real strengths and some real weaknesses as well. It is a tough balancing act to make sure you are rewarding the behaviors in this category while giving very direct feedback in the other categories. You will read more on how to do this later in the chapter.

Low Values, Low Results: Have you specifically discussed the behaviors noted in this category and why you assessed them the way you did? Have you clarified expectations and documented your conversations to make sure you have a shared understanding about the task? Have you considered different roles or tasks that may be a better fit for the employee's competencies, skills, and knowledge where the specific values associated with the task would not be depended upon?

The tough part on this one is managing your own desire to put the employee in another role without ever addressing the low ratings on values. It probably never happens in your company, but, in some places I know, employees rated in this category are moved to another department without the low values assessment ever being addressed in the hopes someone else will handle it.

Low Values, High Results: Have you thought through and clearly defined the *how* associated with the task or responsibility? Have you documented and shared specific behavioral examples with the employee? Have you discussed the impact or consequences of *how* the task is being accomplished? Are you willing to discuss the tasks or responsibilities in this category if there are tasks in other categories?

The biggest stumbling block to discussing the tasks or significant responsibilities in the less-desirable quadrants is our fear that it will demoralize the employee, preventing him or her doing a great job on other tasks. This is a common problem and a fairly inaccurate belief for most people. Employees doing a good job in some tasks or responsibilities almost always want to do a great job overall. Most employees would much rather know what they need to do differently to get even better.

Think about yourself for a moment. Consider a time when you knew you were not quite performing as well as you could. How did you know? Was it better finding out from colleagues and peers in the company, assuming it when you were excluded from certain meetings or projects, or when you got a lower-than-anticipated review at year-end? When we know what we are doing well and why versus where we need to shift, we can usually do something about it. It is the speculation and filling in the blanks that we do that is demoralizing and saps our energy. Shoot straight with employees. You will develop trust and loyalty much faster with this approach than by "sparing" them any negative assessment!

This ongoing, candid, and direct feedback is critical to building a high-performing culture and reaching your destination points effectively. Before we get too far into what works well and what does not work so well with regard to feedback, let's step back for a moment and discuss the focus and function of individual feedback in very general terms.

Feedback

Feedback is the interaction necessary to help an individual or group learn from any recent experience (positive or negative) for the purpose of improving performance and building capabilities. Feedback is providing information about past behavior that may influence future behavior. It comes in many forms, including surveys, e-mails, conversations, break-room chatter, and self-talk. Much of the time our brains fill in the blanks when we do not have data we crave. We simply Make Stuff Up, or, as I like to refer to it, we **MSU**. (As a mother of teenagers, I know a lot about his particular skill set!) We interpret or assume "the truth" based on the selected data we are focusing on around us. If our manager does not greet us with a "hello," we assume we are in trouble or out of the loop. If a leader in the company appears upset, we assume all of our jobs are at stake. Once we decide we have gotten feedback (through whatever source), we constantly look for data that proves we are right. We end up screening out any conflicting data and often create a self-fulfilling cycle.

For this reason alone, *effective* feedback must be ongoing. It is based on positive or negative experiences, direct and honest communication, behaviors, and business relevance, and it is a reflection of what actually occurred versus opinion or speculation. It is specific, constructive, and balanced over time. Some of the less-obvious reasons for providing feedback are (1) more than 70 percent of managers and their employees have different interpretations, and even recollections of the agreements made around performance, and (2) putting these goals and performance measures in writing increases each person's understanding and level of accountability and commitment.

Being good at giving feedback is definitely a set of skills that requires practice. It is not something most people do naturally or with enthusiasm. Even positive feedback is often not delivered according to these criteria. Some leaders and managers assume all employees should know they are doing a good job if they do not hear otherwise. Some feel that praising an employee or team will come across as insincere. Other leaders have great intentions to provide positive feedback, but somehow it never makes it to the top of the to-do list. For whatever reasons, effective feedback is still sorely missing in the workplaces of today. Today, many leaders are of the Traditionalist or Baby Boomer generations, in which praise was infrequent. Giving something that was seldom received is outside of their comfort zone.

Effective feedback should be balanced within every conversation. If your goal is to constantly support others in achieving excellence (as defined by your strategic framework and through your goal-setting process), each interaction you have will move you closer to this goal. If you have some other goal, you should seriously consider why you are a manager or leader in your organization.

There are many myths about effective feedback. Based on the experiences many of us have had with it firsthand from an unskilled manager or leader, you may believe feedback is always a result of negative experiences, vague, manipulative, destructive, judgmental of the person, too general, or given out of context. These are all examples of what effective feedback is *not*.

For feedback to be effective, it relies on trust as a foundation. Feedback should always be business-relevant, tying goals and behaviors back to the strategic framework of the company. If someone's behavior does not have an impact on the success of the company, then it should not matter (unless it is illegal, of course). When you tie the feedback directly to the agreed-upon goals and definition of excellence, it is easier to establish that you are working to be helpful and supportive. Creating business relevance is central to effective feedback, and this is why it is so important to define excellence up front. If I know what excellence looks like, I can measure it and I know when it is being achieved. If I do not know what I am looking for or being asked to do, it is always a guess as to whether I am on the right track. Every small "win" an employee has should be recognizable to him or her even before others acknowledge it. These wins improve confidence and increase engagement.

As our workforces become more diverse, it is increasingly important to define excellence and business relevance to employees. Seemingly simple words have such different meanings to employees. When I talk about behavioral specifics, I cannot rely on just saying something such as, "We want all employees to be customer focused." Customer focused can look dramatically different depending on your culture, your past experiences, your role in the organization, and so on. When you define customer focused as a set of behaviors such as demonstrates sensitivity to customers (both internal and external) and their needs by asking questions and empathizing with individuals, follows through on identified problems until resolved, makes and keeps commitments to customers or advises them when delays are necessary, seeks to exceed customer/client expectations, and adapts approach and style to each customer/client, then I am clear on what you expect. As an employee I can begin to understand what behaviors you want me to exhibit.

Effective feedback must be an intentional, ongoing, daily activity. As a leader or manager, you are providing a great deal of feedback to employees every day, but whether or not it is the feedback you intend to provide is a whole different issue. Without the developed skill set and the time to make it intentional, you are still providing it, but it is most likely being interpreted as something quite different than what you want to communicate. When working to influence the process of feed-back in an organization, I often provide leaders and managers with a set of behaviors and ask them to tell me what it makes them think or feel. (And, more importantly, I ask them to identify if they have ever engaged in the behavior themselves.)

- ❧ You do not take notes during a meeting in which there are assigned deliverables for the attendees.

- ❧ You take phone calls or you answer e-mails during a meeting with an employee.

- ❧ You show up late or cancel team meetings.

- ❧ You postpone a performance review or salary discussion.

- ❧ You do not respond in a timely manner to e-mails from employees.

These seemingly unconscious behaviors are actually send-ing a very clear message, just not the one that promotes re-spect and trust. With the speed in which we operate at work today, these messages are strong because there is often no time to check and see if our interpretation of your behavior is accurate. We simply interpret the behavior (usually in a nega-tive way) and move on. But in moving on, it does not mean the employee has "let it go."

Let's go back and review some of the probable bubbles employees have when we exhibit the behaviors just noted.

➤ You do not take notes during a meeting in which there are assigned deliverables for the attendees.

➤ You take phone calls or you answer e-mails during a meeting with an employee.

No wonder she doesn't hold Gary accountable for his projects, she doesn't take any notes as a reminder to follow up with him....

➤ You show up late or cancel team meetings.

➤ You postpone a performance review or salary discussion.

> How rude. How come he answers e-mails when I am talking? It would be nice to get his full attention sometimes....

> She is late to everything. I guess it's "do as I say, not as I do."

> I just want to get this over with. I wonder if my salary increase will be retroactive.

To counter these likely thought bubbles, behave in a way that is consistent with the values or operating principles of the company. Act intentionally. When you do have to cancel a meeting or conversation for a "truly urgent" matter, tell employees why and reschedule. The key here is the phrase *truly urgent*. If you exhibit these behaviors frequently, you lose credibility when you try to excuse them away. When you have clarity on what excellence looks like, it should help you make the right decisions with regard to urgency and priority. You will know the team meeting is more important than something else competing for your time or, if it is not, you won't schedule it initially.

To counterbalance how the employee interprets your actions, or as a result of engaging in Making Stuff Up (MSU), act in a transparent manner as much as possible. Consider how you would look if your behaviors were highlighted on the evening news or on YouTube. When you need to deliver individual messages, effective feedback should be delivered in a timely manner and leave the employee with no questions as to what you want him or her to continue, start, or stop doing. This helps minimize the MSU that will occur even in the best of circumstances.

Effective feedback is about helping the recipient sustain or improve his or her performance and, consequently, improve his or her self-esteem and morale, and the morale of those with whom the person comes in contact. There are numerous things that can get in the way of providing this timely and effective feedback. For instance, if there is insufficient trust in the relationship between you and an employee, it is unlikely your message will get through. The employee might interpret all your comments has having a hidden agenda or exaggerated. If you have ever failed to give the employee credit for his or her idea, the trust needs to be rebuilt. Perhaps your need to be "right" has prevented you from acknowledging an employee's suggestion or opinion. If you have an underlying, even subtle fear that the employee may be a threat to your job, your feedback may be tainted or withheld.

Providing feedback is often perceived as time-consuming, so managers and leaders put it off in the hopes the employee will get the message (positive or negative) in some other way. As expected, it is easy to get caught up in the tasks of the day—the 100-plus e-mails, phone calls (both office and mobile), instant messages, and video conferencing. It is no longer possible to only respond to these "intrusions" when you are back in the office because portable devices and laptops have become connected to us almost 24 hours a day, seven days a week. With the tremendous technological changes happening so rapidly, most businesses feel the stress of staying ahead of their competition, and this creates an environment of constant urgency that diverts attention from those things we presume can wait—usually the employees and their needs for clarity, direction, information, inspiration, and engagement.

As mentioned earlier, there are four generations of employees in the workforce today. Most of the managers and leader roles are filled with Traditionalists, Baby Boomers, and Generation Xers. Many of them have never received effective feedback themselves, and therefore it is tough to know what to do and how to do it. The concepts of coaching and mentoring have only really come to the forefront in the last decade, while most of the senior managers and executive leaders today started their careers prior to that time. However, because the Millennial generation is more familiar with peer networking through FaceBook and MySpace, peer mentoring and feedback will be more crucial for this generation than earlier ones. Millennials are likely to give feedback up, across, and down, whether it is part of the culture or not, so it is best to prepare them through building skills on doing it well.

There is also a natural discomfort that comes with discussing people's behavior with them, especially if you want it changed. This discomfort is compounded if the employee tends to be aggressive or even successful in getting things done, just not in the way you need them done. It can also be uncomfortable if you only have secondhand data and your instinct or gut tells you it is accurate, but you have a hard time collecting specifics or details.

What Do You Think? Give Me the Score
Assessing the performance of others

The first phase of providing effective feedback is evaluating or assessing the performance of someone else. You need to have a clear sense of what excellence looks like first and then specific examples (preferably firsthand) of the employee's behaviors as compared to the definition of excellence. One of the most common mistakes leaders and managers make is to assess the performance of others based on secret criteria. This happens when the leader or manager has clarity but has forgotten to share it with anyone else. Use the following as a checklist to gauge how well you are doing with assessing others.

> Define excellence and communicate it constantly.

> Observe and note specifics about employees.

   ❧ Look for behaviors as well as impact on others.

   ❧ See what is happening in and across situations.

   ❧ Notice patterns over time.

> Collect data from a variety of sources.

   ❧ Ask your peers and colleagues.

   ❧ Ask for specifics from peers of the employee.

   ❧ Gather customer input, survey scores, and so on.

> Consider any changes or new priorities the employee has been given.

   ❧ Were these changes clear?

   ❧ Were they in addition to other responsibilities or in place of? If they were in addition, how does this affect the expectations or definition of excellence on what was previously assigned?

> Create an initial assessment. "Initial" implies that there may be information pertaining to the assessment or evaluation that you do not currently have. This information may be discovered during conversations with the employee.

Now you are ready to plan when and how you will deliver the specific feedback. This might be as simple as a brief conversation or as part of your ongoing one-on-one conversations.

Common evaluation pitfalls to avoid

Avoiding the following pitfalls is important to accurately assessing an associate's performance.

> **Contrasting**—comparing one employee to another employee instead of to the standards of excellence that link to achieving your strategic plan.

➤ **Fixed Impressions**—allowing an earlier observation to remain fixed in your mind despite data that is different. When you have strong impressions or beliefs about an employee, it is particularly important to look for data that contrasts with your opinion. This process will open you to seeing new things that you are naturally screening out based on your current beliefs.

➤ **Similar to Me**—seeing similarities or differences to yourself and rating the employee accordingly. When you feel a strong connection to someone, especially if it is because you have a similar experience or background, you are much more likely to view them through a positive lens. And the opposite is also true. This is another time when you should diligently look for data that contrasts with your current beliefs about the employee.

➤ **Stereotyping**—ignoring the individuality of a person and seeing him or her as behaving in a way that is supposed to be characteristic of a particular group. We automatically think about this with regard to race and nationality. It also applies to thinking of all people who worked at "X" a certain way or assuming that everyone with a degree in "Y" is similar. Recognize that all employees are unique (just like you are), and think of them that way when you are assessing them.

Because we form mental models very quickly, it can be difficult to avoid these pitfalls. Once we are locked into thinking of someone with a label or mental model (for example, stubborn, slacker, or not very bright), it is hard to see other data even if it exists.

Feedback is a critical skill in coaching and developing others and oneself. The best way to develop your employees into self-reliant achievers is to give them regular feedback on how they are doing on specific tasks and set up a system so they can see for themselves how much progress they are making.

As a leader or manager, you have numerous responsibilities. When you are coaching others on their performances (which is almost always, whether it is intentional or not) your role is to support and facilitate others in reaching the highest standards of team and personal performance as well as assume responsibility for your own performance. Let's review the first part of this equation.

Your role is be to responsible for:

> Facilitating, sharing, collaborating on, and integrating information within the team as well as across teams that can help the team/individual achieve goals.

> Recognizing and reinforcing success, growth, commitment, learning, and change.

> Providing people with honest, meaningful, intentional, and frequent feedback.

> Creating opportunities for associates to experience real responsibility and choices to realize self-motivation.

> Promoting self-awareness and acceptance of responsibility.

> Supporting and facilitating team and individual learning.

> Coaching teams/individuals to learn from mistakes.

Many of your words regarding these responsibilities will be overlooked. Your actions will speak the loudest, so keep in mind the responsibilities you have when you are being coached on performance. Role-model for others what excellence looks like by:

> Identifying your own objectives, measurements, and the skills needed to achieve those objectives using input from others.

- ❧ Seeking your coach's support when setting performance goals or working on performance/ personal development.

- ❧ Asking for feedback from all those with whom you work—your direct reports, peers, customers, suppliers, and vendors.

- ❧ Monitoring your own performance.

- ❧ Providing people with honest, meaningful, and frequent feedback.

- ❧ Participating actively in all phases of the feedback and growth process.

As a receiver of feedback, there are some core skills that you should develop. Listening is the most critical. Listen for what is said to detect key points and issues. Clear your mind when you are receiving feedback. Focus on the moment. Listening is an art, a skill, a discipline, and, like other skills, it requires self-control. You must understand what is involved in listening and develop the necessary techniques to be silent and listen. You must ignore your own needs and concentrate attention on the person speaking. Hearing becomes listening only when you pay attention to what is said and follow it very closely.

Ask yourself if you are listening to your mind more than the speaker's words. Remember that, as soon as someone starts talking to you, your mind is instantly activated as you start processing the words and meanings. Which "noise" are you listening to: the "noise" the other person is making or the "noise" in your own head? Unless you are particularly vigilant, chances are it will be the "noise" in your own head. You can't stop this process, and you don't want to, but just be aware of who you are listening to—you or the speaker? The price of efficient listening is eternal vigilance.

When you exhibit good listening skills, you create an environment in which people are more likely to provide feedback. This supports your employees in trying upward feedback and opens you to receiving more feedback from more sources.

Building Trust

Understanding a person's point of view is integral to building trust and therefore providing effective feedback. People differ in their values, culture, thinking styles, problem-solving methods, education, language, communication abilities, lifestyles, race, gender, expectations, age, and so on. You will benefit more if you realize every person you provide feedback to, or receive feedback from, is first and foremost an individual. The best way to ensure your feedback style recognizes and facilitates differences is to get to know your fellow associates. Tailor the recognition to your employee's needs and personal interests. The key is to do the opposite of the old adage "treat others as you would like to be treated." You should actually treat others as they want to be treated. Consider what areas of their work the employee appears to take great pride in. That is a prime area to reinforce with positive feedback. Does the employee shy away from certain projects or tasks? This is an indication of insecurity with his or her perceived skill level. Can you support his or her growth by finding a mentor to grow that talent?

The following is a general guideline for providing effective feedback.

➤ Inform.

   ❧ Provide information about the strategic planning framework. Discuss the *what* and the *how* the company expects to get to where it wants to go.

➤ **Clarify.**

- ❧ Share what excellence looks like when employees are performing both the *what* and the *how* of their roles.

- ❧ Assist employees in determining priorities and goals.

- ❧ Provide context on how employees' work relates directly to the success of the company and how their performances affects the team.

➤ **Be aware.**

- ❧ Understand that your behaviors speak louder than any words you can say.

➤ **Model.**

- ❧ Act as a role model, demonstrating the desired behaviors.

➤ **Communicate.**

- ❧ Discuss milestones and ongoing changes to any goals or strategies.

➤ **Consider.**

- ❧ Think about the environment you are in and create a comfortable atmosphere when you provide feedback.

➤ **Appreciate.**

- ❧ Consider the feedback you receive as a gift. Sometimes it is just what you want and fits perfectly. Other times, it is the wrong color, the wrong size, and more about the giver than the receiver.

- ❧ Consider the feedback you give as a gift as well. Don't always expect resolution immediately or even appreciation.

➤ **Seek agreement.**

- ❧ When you provide feedback, do it with the intention of creating a shared understanding and agreement on goals, standards, or expectations.

❂ Be open to negotiation if the goal needs to change.

➤ **Adapt.**

❂ Work to understand the other's interests and needs.

❂ Show flexibility with each individual situation.

❂ Have an open mind and release the need to be "right."

❂ Respect the diversity of generations and cultures.

❂ Move outside your comfort zone.

❂ Be creative with new ways of increasing performance levels.

➤ **Collaborate.**

❂ Invite feedback from others.

❂ Demonstrate personal accountability and integrity.

❂ Ask for opinions and solutions.

❂ Share resources.

❂ Build trusting, cooperative relationships with others.

❂ Mentor others.

❂ Avoid playing the "blame game"; focus on solutions.

➤ **Be specific.**

❂ Concentrate on the specific behaviors desired and not on personality traits, as is illustrated in the chart shown on page 179.

Remember that providing feedback on a person's behavior will be ineffective, if not harmful, if it is an opinion or feeling rather than fact. Here are some tips to help avoid giving feedback that is harmful.

❂ Maintain a high sense of awareness of both your emotional state and your intent or motivation as you offer the feedback.

- Be descriptive, not judgmental. Focus on the facts and describe them rather than giving your emotional response.

- Compare expectations to current reality.

- Ask the person you are coaching to compare what he or she had expected to what actually occurred.

- Focus on the results, not on the person.

Behaviors/Actions and Results	Label
Follows through with all promises made from meetings, including delivering reports on time and project assignments on budget. Other departments come to her with questions. Has developed trust and credibility on the team and with others.	Dependable and Reliable
Took initiative to resolve inefficiency of printers and copiers and developed a new integration strategy. Saved office space, reduced repair and maintenance expenses, and increased productivity.	Team Player
Quickly shifted focus on the Website initiative by reprioritizing the project. Integrated multiple teams of programmers by sharing project goals and reassigning responsibilities. Made the deadline and launched new site.	Flexible

In addition, without even realizing it, many managers and leaders have at times unconsciously participated in the following pitfalls. Even if they appear minor, imagine what it might have felt like to be the recipient. Do you recognize these in yourself, or even in your own boss?

> Negative paradigm.

"I have never received positive recognition in my career; therefore, others don't need it."

> Giving mixed messages.

"You did a great job of completing the year-end report on time, but there were several minor errors in one section." Or the dreaded, "This is a great *start*, but..." after the employee has spent days on the project and received no realigning input.

> The recognition is dated and old.

"The presentation you did six months ago was...."

> The recognition is impersonal—for example, a form letter or e-mail.

"The department would like to recognize your efforts."

More or Less: Which Direction Do I Go In?

Now that we have established the importance of feedback and general guidelines for being a giver and receiver of it, let's look more closely at the two types of feedback and the best ways to deliver each type.

There are two primary categories of feedback: (1) *positive and reinforcing*, and (2) *constructive and modifying*.

The power of positive feedback

Praising or positive feedback was noted as one of the secrets in *The One Minute Manager* more than two decades ago. Employees then and today want to know when they are doing a good job. People naturally want to be recognized in a way that is comfortable to them for their contributions to the organization. We instinctively seek input on how we are doing. We look for it all around us. When we do not receive explicit messages about our behaviors, we make up information to fill the void. This information is usually negative. Once we have it set in our minds, we seek to prove ourselves right by looking for more evidence that we are about to be fired, get demoted, or get a bad performance review.

Spending the time to reinforce desired behaviors pays off in many ways. In addition to the obvious value of keeping people aligned to the strategic plans of the company, there is an intrinsic value in positive feedback. Not only can it help motivate an employee to continue to put in that extra effort, it can also be successful at helping them through a rough time when their confidence may be low as a result of a less-than-favorable project outcome. Showing respect through positive feedback in the everyday work environment can also have a tremendous impact on the level at which an employee or a team functions. Just by being aware of an employee's time constraints, and beginning a conversation with "When you get a minute,..." is a simple way to show the employee you respect him, his time, and his level of focus.

When to provide positive feedback

Praise employees when they:

- Go beyond the duties expected of them.
- Produce more than the amount produced by any predecessor.
- Turn a particularly difficult customer into a promoter.
- Reach new levels of accuracy.

- Develop or contribute significantly to another colleague.

- Create a new process, product, or approach.

- Present an idea for doing something differently (even if the idea does not get implemented).

- Do an exceptional job presenting or influencing internally or externally.

- Excel at a presentation.

- Participate significantly in a community event on behalf of the company.

Positive feedback or praise must be sincere. Setting up a system to just rotate your feedback to different team members defeats the purpose of effective praising. Don't praise someone for showing up on time or getting the basics of the job done. Don't praise someone because you are feeling guilty about providing constructive feedback and you think you need to cushion it. The "sandwich" approach to feedback was popular when Traditionalists and Baby Boomers were the only two generations in the workforce. Leaders and managers were taught to say something positive, sneak in something you want done differently, and then end on a positive note. Generation Xers saw through this strategy and just wondered aloud what the hidden agenda was every time they got positive feedback. They kept waiting for the other shoe to drop when their managers said something positive. Millennials are so accustomed to direct and often brutal feedback that they certainly do not want or need constructive feedback snuck into a conversation.

How to provide positive feedback effectively

Don't make this harder than it really is. If it is genuine and follows these basic parameters, it is the easiest thing you will do all day, and you will feel great doing it.

➤ Immediate.

Give the recognition as soon as possible after the event. No matter what the expectations, positive feedback and recognition meet very important human needs. When done well, it leads to:

- More of the desired behavior.
- Improved work quality.
- Increased accountability.
- A higher-performing work environment.
- Increased morale.

➤ Specific.

State specifically what the associate did that met or exceeded your expectations. Our language is inexact. We often use the same words to mean very different things, so be as specific as possible in your feedback. Getting clear messages on behaviors is critical to deepening our understanding.

➤ Impactful.

Tell the associate how the event or behavior affected you, the team, or the organization.

➤ Encouraging.

Continued desired performance needs to be encouraged so that other messages, often made-up, do not take the employee off track.

➤ Sincere.

Demonstrate your sincerity with your body language and your words. End with a smile and a handshake.

Match the reward to the employee

Research shows that employees are motivated in their work by a combination of three general factors:

1. Affiliation.

   Having a connection to the organization and/or its public reputation is important to many employees. Personal relationships with individuals within the organization also fill the affiliation needs.

2. Development.

   Being provided opportunities to grow skills and gain new experiences is a strong motivator to many employees.

3. Financial.

   Salaries, bonuses, and benefits that compensate an individual for his or her work contributions and time vary dramatically as a motivator for employees. Salary is not usually a determinant in employees leaving your organization, but providing financial incentives can support getting higher levels of performance and directly driving desired behaviors.

Although these categories are generally applicable, the degree to which each one plays out for an individual will vary tremendously. In fact, no two employees will have the exact same expectation. Rewards, like feedback, should not be distributed based on "treat others the way you want to be treated." Equal does not mean it has to be exactly the same for each employee. Not everyone finds value in all types of recognition. One person may appreciate public applause; another may prefer a private thank-you note. Just as you must understand the individuality of each employee with regard to skill level and competencies, so must you be able to recognize each person's individuality when it comes to appropriate rewards. Take a few minutes to think about the differences in style and approach of your direct reports. When rewards are customized to each employee, their impact on motivation and retention can increase significantly.

Consider the following when deciding on the appropriate reward:

➤ Whether the individual might like public or private recognition.

  ❧ What have you observed about the interactions in meetings?

  ❧ Is the person more of an introvert, or does he or she always speak up and contribute?

  ❧ Does the person embarrass easily, or is he or she the one making jokes in the office?

➤ What the employee enjoys (for example, cards, picture frame, gift card, flowers, and chocolate).

  ❧ Notice the employee's work space. What types of things does he or she display?

  ❧ Where does the person tend to dine at lunch or stop in the morning for coffee? A gift card to a favorite place demonstrates that you are observant and thoughtful.

➤ How important it is to the individual's career path/ desires that others know.

  ❧ Are the behaviors indicative of someone on the fast track within the organization?

  ❧ Does the employee need visibility in the organization to get the next promotion or significant project assignment?

Forms of recognition
Start Small:

➤ Make it a habit to say, "Thank You," often. Make sure you change it up a bit so that it doesn't become routine like asking, "How are you doing?" Specify what you are thanking employees for to maintain a sense of sincerity.

➤ Give compliments and be specific.

➤ Say, "Good morning," by name.

➤ Recognize individual accomplishments with a short e-mail note or comment in a team meeting.

➤ Inform the employee's boss of your recognition.

➤ Write a handwritten note of appreciation.

➤ Leave a sticky note with a snack thanking the person for his or her efforts.

➤ Leave a voicemail that the employee will receive first thing in the morning.

➤ Give small gifts such as stress balls, desk toys, and motivational calendars.

Grow Bigger:

➤ Orchestrate a thank-you letter or e-mail from upper management (see template on page 188).

➤ Send flowers to the employee's office or home.

➤ Give the person an increase or change in responsibility and authority.

➤ Increase flexibility of work hours and/or occasional comp time.

➤ Assign the employee to a visible project or one that will really stretch his or her current skill set.

➤ Allow the individual to observe a team or project that would be a big promotion (and thus a learning opportunity to observe).

➤ Make a highly visible parking space reserved for Teammate of the Month (or Quarter).

➤ Arrange for your manager or a senior manager to take your group out to lunch or dinner to celebrate a team accomplishment.

➤ Give your employee a relevant book inscribed with a message from upper management recognizing his or her accomplishment.

➤ Create and implement a team, department-specific, or overall organization recognition program. It is just as important for employees and teams to recognize each other as it is for a manager to acknowledge good work.

    ✎ Consider establishing a "Caring Credits" program in which each employee receives a minimum of three blank cards at the beginning of the month. Employees then acknowledge their colleagues for going above and beyond their job requirements by writing a note to a colleague on each card. When designing these cards, take advantage of the front side for sharing monthly inspirational quotes. The cards could be submitted to the human resources department, and at the end of the month the person who receives the most nominations earns the title of Employee of the Month. All of the cards can then be inserted in each employee's envelope with their paychecks at the beginning of the next month or distributed via interoffice mail so they can see the praise they received from their coworkers. Practices such as these force employees to pause and write down their positive feedback. This creates a powerful habit.

    ✎ Find some wall space in the office and pick a Friday afternoon to engage with the employees in creating their own (and *your* own) "What's Great?" boards. These can be as simple as a large easel page that has the employee's name at the top with "What's Great?" written on it. The purpose of the board is for the employee to write a brief note or sentence about something great that occurred that week. The notes can be professional or personal achievements, or incidents. Encourage individuals to also contribute to each other's boards and watch how easily they begin to add to the boards on their own without weekly prompting. The different handwritings and colored markers used will also brighten up the workspace, and visitors and other departments will stop by just to see what is new on the boards.

Recognition e-mail template

To: *Employee Deserving Recognition*
CC: *Team Members*
Subject: *Your contributions on XYZ project*

Congratulations and a sincere thank you for your recent contributions (completing/launching) XYZ project. The challenges involving (deadlines, vendors, changing requirements, etc.) were formidable. Your professionalism, dedication, and solution-orientated thinking helped keep the project on track.

It seems our projects like XYZ always teach us valuable lessons. At next month's team meeting, can you talk to the group for five minutes or so on what you learned from the experience? I am sure your success will be a great lesson-learned for all of us.

Again, congratulations and thank you on a job well done!

Constructive and Modifying Feedback
When to realign performance

There are times when an employee is not operating within the boundaries of defined excellence. At these times, it is critical to provide constructive feedback so that course correction can occur right away. The only purpose of constructive feedback should be to modify future behaviors. Constructive feedback should not be delivered as a punishment for "bad" behavior. It should not be done in anger or retaliation.

Performance problems can have many causes and take many forms. Sometimes it is a minor issue that is inadvertently getting in the way. Other times it is a flagrant violation of company values or operating principles. Confronting any type of less-than-excellent performance is one of the hardest management tasks. "I don't want to deal with the employee's anger," "But the problem existed before I took over the department," "I don't want to be the bad guy," and "It's really no big deal. I am probably one of the only people who even notices" are some rationales leaders and managers use to avoid what they think will be confrontational conversations.

Yet less than fully-satisfactory performance must be addressed before it becomes a major problem—for the benefit of the company, the work group, the manager, and the associate. It is the manager's job to recognize, candidly discuss, and help resolve performance problems. Poor performance often affects more than just the manager and the poor performer.

The discomfort involved in confronting someone with feedback of poor performance sometimes encourages managers to look the other way and hope the situation will improve by itself. However, addressing in the early stages provides the following benefits:

- ❧ Early action will often avoid broader impact.

- ❧ Early conversations may surface new information of which the manager was unaware. Managerial intervention may be able to address issues outside the employee's control.

- ❧ Conversations can often take on a more coaching tone ("How can I help you with this?") as opposed to a more disciplinary tone.

How to provide constructive feedback

The following behaviors will support you in having these tough conversations:

➤ Be direct and supportive.

Effective providers of feedback know how to be clear and focused with their comments, while at the same time being sensitive and respectful to the recipient. Keep in mind what the impact of your discussion may be.

➤ Give behavioral examples and data.

Clear feedback is full of specifics. State specifically what was done, when it was done, in what context it occurred, and what impact it had.

➤ Expose your thinking.

Consciously state what data you observed, what assumptions you made, and what conclusions you drew. This will support the employee in understanding your thinking processes as well as enable her to refute any faulty data.

➤ Solicit reaction.

Ensure that the employee feels open to responding to the feedback by asking him for his thoughts or view on what happened. Creating a two-way dialogue will support a healthy relationship for coaching and improvement. Ask questions and seek common understanding.

➤ Be open to new information.

Be careful not to go into the discussion with your conclusions set in stone. New information may change the way you view certain behaviors.

➤ **Stay focused and on point.**

Ensure that neither person uses distractions and tangents to avoid having the conversation.

➤ Get a commitment to action.

Feedback can be useless unless the receiver agrees and makes a commitment to modify the behavior. In addition, constructive feedback is even more likely to be misinterpreted than other forms, so summarize your feedback and expectations of future action in writing following the session.

The brief worksheet that follows can help you prepare to discuss a performance problem while it is in the early stages. Answering the questions that follow will help you clarify your views of the employee's performance and will give you data for discussion when you meet with the employee to resolve a performance problem. It is a thinking and analysis guide designed to support you in preparing.

1. What is unsatisfactory about the employee's performance? That is, what behaviors and/or results are not being accomplished or what performance requirements are not being met?

2. How long has it been a problem?

3. Think about two situations in which the individual had an opportunity to accomplish the goals in an appropriate way but did not do so. What happened?

4. What were the situations? What led up to them? Who was involved?

5. What did the associate say? Do? (Get firsthand information, as if a videotape recorder might capture it. Stay away from second- or third-hand information and opinion!)

6. What was produced? What impact did it have on others? On the organization? What was unsatisfactory?

7. What is your perception of the cause of the problem? Is it a competencies, skills, or knowledge problem? A style/values problem? A motivation problem? A resource problem?

8. What role have you played?

9. What specifically needs to be changed in order for performance to be fully satisfactory? During the feedback session, wait for the employee to respond with suggestions during your conversation and be prepared with suggestions of your own.

10. What will you use as evidence to show that the behavior has improved? During your conversation with the employee, ask the employee what measurement should be used to determine incremental wins or milestones.

11. What support are you willing to give? What resources may the employee need to make the necessary changes?

Just as you did not learn to walk or ride a bike the first time out, it will take a few tries to change or modify an employee's behavior or learn a new skill. Patience and respect for yourself and the employee are essential during this process.

Depending on the duration and severity of a performance problem, leaders and managers will generally play two roles in addressing performance issues: coach and disciplinarian.

In the early stages of a performance issue, leaders and managers should assume a coaching role. At this point, the focus should be on helping the associate to succeed. Focus the individual on understanding the objectives and on clarifying *what* needs to be done including *how* to do it. In these scenarios, you should share the notes you have gathered. Typically nothing formal needs to be written up at this stage, but the leader or manager should keep notes.

When coaching fails to move performance to the desired level, you must shift into the disciplinarian role. When in this role, you must document discussions, expectations, and consequences. In most cases, such documentation will be progressive in nature, building to a final resolution. It should clearly state expectations and results of failure to meet these objectives so that if/when you have to move to the next step, the individual is fully aware of the consequences of noncompliance.

A Coach provides...	A Disciplinarian focuses on...
Direction and guidance	Initiating corrections
Suggestions	Ensuring compliance
Insight	Adherence to policies, procedures, and standards of excellence
Motivation	Explaining consequences
Perspective on impact	Details of what must be done
Big-picture thinking	Ensuring good of the team and the company

And another thing...

Almost all feedback is also complicated by the reactions we have and the diversions that stop us from productive conversations. When we give and when we receive feedback, sometimes we appear as if we are on the stage performing in an interesting production. Sometimes our fears, uncertainties, and doubts about feedback make us very uncomfortable. We react in interesting ways. See if you recognize the following characters.

"...the Oscar Goes To..."

Leading Actors (providing feedback):
➤ **Magician.**

Disguises the feedback and the receiver is left guessing what the real message was. This often occurs when the manager is afraid of hurting the associate's feelings or is worried about not being liked himself. The leader or manager slips in the negative comments when you aren't looking, but the receiver walks away wondering what the show was all about.

➤ **Corporate Enforcer.**

"Just doing my job and delivering the message; it's not like I wanted to or that I even believe it is necessary." The actor gets off the hook for having any negative thoughts or opinions about the behaviors of the employee and protects his or her good-guy status.

➤ **Hero.**

This manager plays the part of the protector while delivering the feedback as if he or she is only there to help. The manager then steps in and offers to resolve it him- or herself. The leader or manager may pretend that he or she does not even agree with the feedback while backpedaling out of the discussion.

➤ **Interrogator.**

This actor asks a series of tough questions, trying to get the employee to figure out what he or she might not have done well. The Interrogator never provides the answer or specifics on behaviors.

➤ **Game Show Host.**

This feedback discussion includes a guessing game in which the employee doesn't really know what the manager is thinking, but is expected to play the game nonetheless. At the end, the employee is scratching her head and wondering what it was all about.

Supporting Actors (receiving feedback):
➤ **Victim.**

The receiver is so hard on him- or herself that the feedback is taken way out of context. Often a victim will take the feedback as if it is a condemnation of him or her as a person, and overreact.

> **Sheep Herder.**

This actor believes there is safety in numbers and finds (or at least identifies) many other employees who are engaging in the same behavior, thus justifying his or her own actions. This is a perfect way to avoid responsibility and accountability for personal performance, and it can be intimidating to a feedback-giver because it feels as if the whole organization is suddenly against you.

> **Ex-spouses.**

Actors in this scene each blame the other person for anything less than perfection. Both the giver and the receiver of the feedback become defensive and stop listening altogether.

> **Con (Wo)man.**

The actor in this scene creates tangents and diversions to take the feedback-giver off track by bringing up other projects, issues, or behaviors.

Do any of these casts of characters remind you of anyone? Hopefully you do not have the advanced acting skills required to participate in these scenes yourself. If you do, really look at what behavior is getting in the way of your valuable feedback and try to develop a better understanding of why you do it so you can be more effective.

In order to stop and eject this movie, there needs to be some honesty at work. Recognize the role that is being played and stop the discussion. When you realize that the role is just a way of avoiding fears, one of the best things you can do is show empathy towards the other person (and yourself) and get refocused on the current issue.

Feedback Summary

Providing and receiving effective feedback is not easy. It takes practice in a safe environment—one where leaders, managers, and employees believe that the intentions are good, where feedback is expected and appreciated, where integrity between words and actions is valued and rewarded. Feedback does not stand alone. It is a significant component of your overall work culture. It is nearly impossible to package up feedback and launch a process without looking at the entire culture. I often say to clients, "Your culture or system produces exactly what it is set up to produce." If you want to change whether or not feedback is being done well and supports the alignment of individual performance with business goals, you have to do more than just launch a feedback initiative or project. You have to change the culture or system in a sustainable manner. Feedback is a result of numerous beliefs and norms throughout an organization and unless underlying beliefs or thought bubbles change, behaviors will remain the same.

Chapter 4 Executables

➤ Provide ongoing, effective feedback to maintain high performance and keep the organization focused on the overall destination.

➤ Individualize your feedback to accommodate the four generations in the workforce.

⟐ Are you providing feedback the same way for your Traditionalists and Baby Boomers as you are for Generation Xers and Millennials?

➤ Push yourself to examine what is getting in the way of feedback in your organization.

⟐ Think through your current system or culture.

⟐ Are leaders and managers conducting conversations?

⟐ Do team members offer their input and ideas to others?

❧ Is it okay to give advice to colleagues and your boss?

➤ Consider that both *what* an associate does and *how* he or she does it is critical to performance excellence and reaching your destination points.

   ❧ Where do your employees fit in the Values and Results Matrix (found on page 158)?

   ❧ With which quadrant are you spending most of your time?

   ❧ What can you do as their manager to maintain or improve their performance?

➤ Re-examine your feedback before you give it to verify that it is business relevant, tying goals and behaviors back to the strategic framework of the company.

➤ Consider the following guidelines when providing effective feedback.

   ❧ Inform.

   ❧ Clarify.

   ❧ Be aware.

   ❧ Model.

   ❧ Communicate.

   ❧ Consider.

   ❧ Appreciate.

   ❧ Seek agreement.

   ❧ Adapt.

   ❧ Collaborate.

   ❧ Be specific.

➤ Provide effective, positive feedback by making sure it is immediate, specific, impactful, encouraging, and sincere.

➤ Follow the same guidelines when providing rewards. Remembering that a great manager is also thoughtful and sincere with his or her rewards. Match the reward to the individual. Be interested and observant, and you will find this is easy to do.

➤ Address less-than-fully satisfactory performance before it becomes a major problem—for the benefit of the company, the work group, the manager, and the associate.

   ❧ Be direct and supportive.

   ❧ Give behavioral examples and data.

   ❧ Expose your thinking.

   ❧ Solicit reaction.

   ❧ Be open to new information.

   ❧ Avoid distractions and tangents.

➤ Get a commitment to **action**.

Chapter 5

Leveraging and Learning: Measuring and Ongoing Improvement

The job of being a leader and manager today definitely takes more than a minute! As you have no doubt noted in the first four chapters of this book, a lot has changed in the past 25 years! However, a few of the basics are still critical. They just look and feel differently today. The world moves faster and is more connected. Businesses come and go at lightning speed. Balancing the needs and expectations of four generations at work increases the challenges. Responding to globalization and the increasing rate of complexity and change can feel overwhelming.

To keep up, a leader and manager today has to excel at:

Getting back to basics

➤ Make strategic planning a way of life in your organization.

- ❧ Use the strategic planning framework to drive what you do and where you focus your energies.

- ❧ Embed ongoing strategic planning in your processes. Constantly check for internal and external forces that may affect where you are going, *what* you need to do, and *how* you need to do it.

- ❂ Organize your day so you reach your destination, as well as inform, inspire, and engage others to get there too.

➤ Communicate constantly about your strategic-planning framework.

- ❂ Inform employees of where you are going, and where you are today, and keep them updated.

- ❂ Set clear expectations of what excellence looks like.

- ❂ Expose the *why* behind your decisions.

- ❂ Establish individual goals linked to the company's strategic-planning framework.

- ❂ Inspire employees by presenting a compelling picture of what the future looks like.

- ❂ Engage employees continuously by asking about progress and highlighting accomplishments.

➤ Build a high-performing culture that supports your strategies.

- ❂ Consider *what* it will take and *how* you will get to your destination points, and communicate both constantly.

- ❂ Measure what matters and what employees can relate to in their jobs every day.

- ❂ Encourage ownership behaviors in employees.

- ❂ Remain vigilant about reviewing external and internal forces that may affect your strategies.

- ❂ Give people what they need to be successful. Set yourself and everyone in the organization up for success.

- ❂ Review organization processes and systems to be sure they are aligned with where you say you are going.

➤ Provide continuous feedback.

- ❂ Consider values and results.

- ❂ Build trust through understanding others.

● Link to rewards and recognition.

● Deal with problem performers.

To complement these actions, put in place the right measures and processes for measuring.

Measure It: Keep Track

Remember the old adage, what gets measured, gets done? Well, what does not get measured may still be getting done in your organization as well. Unfortunately, it may not be what you want done or what gets you to your destination. You must continually help employees gain clarity with regard to what they should still be working on. Organizational needs are constantly changing. Goals that were set in January may be out of date by March if significant external or internal forces have created a new environment in which you operate. As changes happen, managers and leaders must work with employees to stay clear on what the current priorities are. Just because a project was announced and set as a top priority in February does not mean it will remain that way for an entire year or several years.

When effective goal-setting is done, combined with a method to track progress and identify obstacles, it contributes to success and bottom-line results. Regularly tracking progress against performance goals and objectives also provides the opportunity to recognize and reward employees, which contributes to job satisfaction and productivity. As was mentioned earlier, employees want to feel successful, do well at their jobs, and feel they are making valuable contributions. In order to ensure this, you must track progress and constantly communicate it.

Use your breakthrough model as the basis for creating an ongoing tracking and measurement system. Your organization will continually provide clues and cues as to whether or not individuals and teams are on track. The most obvious will be in the results achieved and/or milestones met. But as we

More Than a Minute

covered many times throughout this book, do not focus solely on results. The *how* of getting there is equally important. However, you will only notice your progress if you have measures in place and they are getting looked at on an ongoing basis.

Measure the right things.

Remember to measure against standards of excellence and the desired state. Clearly note in your destination points what it looks like when you get to where you are going. Plainly define what behaving in the desired manner looks like. What would others see if they observed the company going about its day-to-day work? And remember the pink elephant! If you want everyone in the organization focused on customer retention, measure retention versus customer turnover or churn. If profits are important, measure profitable revenue growth versus revenue alone, measure employee retention versus employee turnover.

Measure the right number of things.

Focus on three to five key strategies. These are the areas of focus across the organization. Too many strategies and energies become dispersed and unfocused, so you really have no strategies. Too few strategies and most day-to-day activities won't support it, meaning you really have none. Employees will just continue doing what they have always done—working hard, but not necessarily working on the right things.

You will have determined your core initiatives through building your breakthrough models. What are the significant projects or initiatives that must occur to move you from your current state to your desired state? These core initiatives sometimes correlate to one strategy, but sometimes initiatives support multiple strategies. It is not important that there is a one-to-one relationship of initiative to strategy. What is important is that each significant initiative in the organization does support at least one strategy.

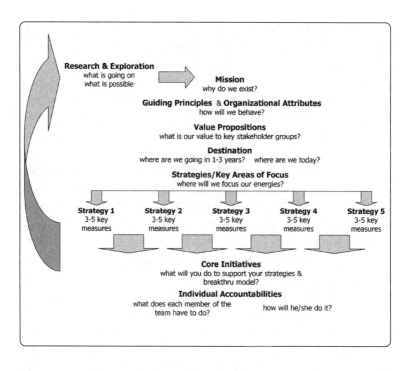

Today, almost all employees work hard. Most people do so believing they are working on the right things that will make a difference to the organization. However, if you do not remain vigilant in aligning core initiatives with your strategies, you will find that time, money, and other resources are spent working on the wrong things. For one of my clients, we do an exercise once a year to examine all the significant initiatives in the company. We call it "The Plate Exercise." Approximately three months after the strategic-planning framework has been completed and communicated, we spend time examining "what is on the plate" and "what should fall off the plate" as far as significant projects and initiatives. This helps make sure the appropriate number of resources are allocated to the highest value activities.

204 ▶

This exercise forces the company to refocus efforts on the right things and make tough choices about what employees should start, stop, and continue doing. The exercise is especially useful when your organization's leader is an "idea person," constantly coming up with more things to do than the resources of the organization can possibly support. It provides a structure and a process to help you stay on the path to your destination, or to adjust it knowingly so new destination points can be communicated and energy can shift throughout the company. In many organizations today, there is a plethora of ideas and possibilities, but resources are stretched too thin. The highest value projects may not be getting the attention they need.

To do "The Plate Exercise," each initiative is ranked according to its strategic value. Strategic value will have a definition unique to your strategic planning framework. The following are some examples I have used with clients. These statements describe the two ends of the scale or continuum. You might use a numeric rating such as 1 through 5 or a qualitative rating such as critical, important, unknown, or even a simple high, medium, or low rating. The value in this exercise is not in the precision of ratings. The value is in uncovering all the projects and initiatives that employees are working on so you can make informed choices about where resources should be invested.

For Business Initiatives (including product/service enhancements):

➤ Consider the link to core strategies for:

   ❧ Direct support of key strategy ⇔ indirect/no clear link to current strategy (could be longer term).

   ❧ Necessary for long-term growth ⇔ nice to have, but not critical for ongoing growth.

   ❧ Necessary for short-term revenue capture ⇔ nice to have, but not critical in short term.

- ❧ Clarity of project (requirements, outputs, costs, and revenue impact) ⇔ fuzzy project requirements at present.

- ❧ Known impact to revenue ⇔ unknown or unclear impact on revenue.

- ❧ Clear owner/sponsor ⇔ unclear owner/sponsor.

- ❧ Delay in project has immediate and significant revenue impact ⇔ delay in project has no immediate or significant revenue impact.

- ❧ Confirmed customer/consumer need ⇔ speculative/ addresses more general issues (versus known need).

➤ Determine customer impact/satisfaction

- ❧ Transparent to customer ⇔ disruption/inconvenience to customer.

- ❧ Directly addresses targeted/high-impact customer issue ⇔ addresses longer-term customer concern.

➤ Prioritization considerations

- ❧ Annual operating plan is dependent on revenue production in near term ⇔ longer-term revenue impact.

- ❧ Critical to core business operations ⇔ important, but not necessary immediately.

- ❧ Resources in place/project underway ⇔ new/additional resources required/project not started.

For Operational Improvements:
➤ Necessary for long-term growth ⇔ nice to have, but not critical for ongoing growth.

➤ Clarity of project (requirements, outputs, costs, and revenue impact) ⇔ fuzzy project requirements at present.

➤ Known impact to revenue ⇔ unknown or unclear impact on revenue.

➤ Clear owner/sponsor ⇔ unclear owner/sponsor.

➤ Delay in project has immediate and significant revenue impact ⇔ delay in project has no immediate or significant revenue impact.

➤ Confirmed customer/consumer need ⇔ speculative/ addresses more general issues (versus known need).

For Daily Operations:
➤ Critical to core business operations ⇔ important, but not necessary immediately.

➤ Resources in place/project underway ⇔ new/additional resources required/project not started.

➤ Ongoing operations necessity ⇔ longer term operational excellence.

Other value scales or considerations:

Scale type	Rating	To consider
Strategic	1 (high) to 5 (low)	**Initiative will have impact on achieving objectives including:** ► Market penetration ► Market share capture/retention ► Customer acquisition/retention ► Confirmed customer need is addressed (versus speculative or incremental improvements) ► Direct support of a key strategy for current year ► Necessity for long-term growth (versus a nice to have) **Other considerations:** ► Clarity of objectives, including requirements, outputs, costs, and revenue impact ► Clear ownership and accountability of overall initiative as well as components ► Delay in project/initiative has immediate and significant impact

Scale type	Rating	To consider
Revenue	1 (high) to 5 (low)	**Initiative will contribute directly to <u>revenue</u>, including:** ► Known time frame ► Known direct link between initiative and revenue ► Delay in initiative will have significant revenue impact
Contribution to profit margin	1 (high) to 5 (low)	**Initiative will contribute directly to <u>profit margin</u>, including:** ► Known time frame ► Known direct link between initiative and revenue ► Delay in initiative will have significant profit implications
Headcount	Yes/No	► Resources required are in place or are on track to be in place in short term ► Resources required are not in place currently and no source has been identified and confirmed to obtain them ► Key skill gaps exist in the organization and no source has been identified and confirmed
Talent constraints	Skill Quantity	► Note specific skill sets missing that are required to complete the initiative ► Note number of additional resources required to complete the initiative
Priority	1 (high) to 10 (low)	► The operating plan is depending on this initiative for revenue and/or contribution to profit in the near term ► The initiative is critical to core business operations ► The project/initiative is well underway and is staffed adequately to deliver

Choose whatever scales and measures work in your organization and rate each project. Then decide if you have the resources to do them all well. If you do not, lower value initiatives should be halted or abandoned. If you do have all the resources, link each initiative or project to your strategies and make sure you are making progress across all strategies. Sometimes one strategy is more compelling than another and our resources unintentionally get lopsided in supporting it.

Measuring Organizational Progress

Leaders and managers today need a simple, practical way to measure and report progress toward the destination points, including creating a context for excellence. Imagine watching a sports event in which they did not keep score, or buying stock with no dollar value to measure its worth. Employees want to know where things stand. To keep them engaged, you have to constantly communicate progress and barriers.

Many people think of measurement as a tool to control behavior or micromanage others. A scorecard can actually be helpful in clarifying the strategy and goals, as well as managing alignment across individuals, departments, and initiatives. When used effectively, the scorecard becomes a communication vehicle, not a constraint for employees. It provides a variety of views into the business and helps you maintain focus across all the important indicators. Think about flying an airplane. You need to know where you are going, and you need indicators to tell you how you are doing along the way. You can't just look at one gauge when you fly. Airspeed, altitude, and direction are all important. Fuel, weight, and oil indicators are essential too. When you take your eyes off one of them, you almost always make an adjustment that affects the others. It is pretty easy to see why constantly looking across all the indicators is important to the safety of your flight.

Your scorecard makes many of the elements of your destination points very real by noting them in tangible, near-term, measurable ways. It also helps further refine expectations and standards of excellence. A scorecard can also produce intangible benefits. When shared with external partners such as bankers, investors, and suppliers, it demonstrates business discipline and can establish credibility. Internally it generates greater awareness and understanding of all the company's pieces and parts. It can encourage interaction among managers, teams, and departments that contribute to common goals. Accountability and responsibility become clear across the company and there is a greater sense of ownership when individuals can see how what they do each day contributes to the overall progress of the company. It also makes clear if there are troubled areas of the business that need more attention or resources.

There is a variety of approaches you can take to build a scorecard. Your scorecard tells a story and sends a loud message to employees about what you really think is important. I have worked with clients who have a strategy of becoming an "employer of choice." The only problem is that they do not measure or look at any indicators of progress toward this lofty statement. Your measures are going to be viewed through the lens of "let's see what they really think here...," so make sure they are linked to all strategies and include creating a culture of high performance.

Your scorecard will certainly contain key financial metrics. Choose three or four. These are usually revenue, profit margin, or operating expenses as a percentage of revenue. In addition to the typical measures, try to choose some leading indicators such as number of customers signed up or new employees hired. These leading indicators forecast your future performance. They provide insight into what is to come. You should have a measure associated with all the categories on your destination modeling. The measure answers the question: "How will we know if we are moving toward our destination?"

Another way to design metrics is to think about your stakeholders and design measures that mean something to them. For instance, what do your customers or clients care about? What matters most to employees? ...to suppliers or vendors? ...to investors? Go back and review your stakeholder value propositions to determine what metrics might be important to each group. This look can often provide a good view of culture-oriented metrics. What do employees really want from your organization? Do they want to learn and develop? Do they want to be challenged every day? Do they want direct, candid, and timely feedback? Measure what your key stakeholders care most about.

Yet another approach is to use the following table to outline, by strategy, what your scorecard looks like. Answer the question(s) noted in each section and you will quickly see how the pieces fit together.

Strategy	Key Initiatives and Commitments
Are we focused on the right thing?	► What will we do by when? ► Who is on the hook for results?
Key Measures (including targets and/or destination points) ► How will we know if we are making progress?	**Risks and Mitigating Actions** ► What are our risks? ► How can we minimize them?

This approach keeps everything on one or a few pages so that it is easy for everyone to see the links between the strategies, the initiatives or commitments, the measures, and the risks or barriers. It also outlines very clearly who is going to do what by when. This encourages accountability throughout the organization. Lastly, the approach develops a more proactive view by forcing you to consider risks and managing them before they become a problem.

Whichever one of these tools you use, make sure you are using it in your ongoing communications with employees. Talk about it constantly. You can-not overcommunicate about your strategic planning frame-work, and your team and in-dividual goals! Your ongoing behavior in this regard will make it evident that you are steadfast in getting the com-

> **Key Operating Practice:** Choose a tool that will work in your organization and that you will commit to using.

pany to where it needs to go. You can say you are a hundred times, but your behavior will speak much more loudly and have a more lasting impact on employees.

Report progress as broadly as possible within the organi-zation each month. Report challenges or barriers as well. Note how you are adjusting timelines or other elements. If you do not, people will MSU (Make Stuff Up) and create much worse scenarios about why you are not getting to where you need to go. The less made-up thought bubbles, the better!

As you progress toward your destination points, there will be surprises. These will include external forces that you could not possibly have known about ahead of time. They will also include internal forces, such as unspoken beliefs, that underlie and undermine stated goals. Your own belief that plans will go smoothly and easily lead to your destination points could get in the way of managing the current state. Expectations that plans will not require fundamental organizational changes are dangerous. As mentioned previously, do not underestimate how much change might be required in the organization and how hard change typically is.

A belief that I see in most organizations is that once the plan is written, it will get done exactly as intended. It is a funny notion considering how most plans end up in binders on someone's credenza or shelf. Do not mistake a written plan for reality. Constant two-way communication is absolutely essential to making adjustments based on the unfolding reality of your organization and environment. As a leader or manager, know that you do not know how everything will turn out, even if you have a beautifully documented plan. Be prepared to adjust, and then communicate those adjustments, as necessary.

Another belief or bubble that "we just have to execute" drives us to assume we have commitment and aligned actions across the company. It is common for tasks to slip and obligations to be missed, often because of the demands of old and obsolete processes. The past is almost always compelling because people at least think they understand what happened and why. There is some comfort in the knowing, even if we do not like it. It is important to make sure that the future is more compelling than the past, and that you have explicit commitment across the organization.

The following are a few questions you might consider as you measure your progress toward your destination points.

- ❧ In what specific ways do your breakthrough model actions and reality differ?

- ❧ How does the expected pace of getting to your destination points compare to the actual pace?

- ❧ What indicators are vital to assessing your relationships with your markets?

- ❧ What measurements do you regularly make to assess all of your stakeholder relationships?

- ❧ What were the real reasons for your past successes and failures?

- ❧ What proportion of your organization's resources is focused on maintaining and enhancing the status quo versus new initiatives?

❧ How much time do you spend leading and promoting the destination points?

❧ What new initiatives have you started in the past year? What initiatives have you stopped?

❧ Do near-term problems and opportunities consume everyone's time and preempt your longer-term progress?

❧ Do you have clear champions who will keep others focused on making progress for each significant initiative?

❧ Are there consequences for missing deadlines or other obligations?

Constant focus on both strategy and implementation is the job of leaders and managers today. This is one of the most significant differences from 25 years ago. Speed, the rate of change, and the access to information have created a whole new set of demands that require your daily attention. To help you do a great job today, use the tool most suited for you (such as a to-do list, a sticky note reminder, or an automated task ping) so that you develop the sense of urgency around strategy and focused implementation as you do around all the other "emergencies" that you have throughout the day.

> **Key Operating Practice:** Balance your energy across strategy and execution. Defining strategy gets you moving in the right direction. You will stall quickly and perhaps even end up somewhere else if you don't spend energy executing as well.

I like to use the following approach, but adapt it to best suit your preferred style.

➤ Plan out your time for the week.

Segment it into blocks (for example, collecting data on strategy X, hands-on work on initiative Y, feedback sessions, customer meetings, and internal or external communication events).

➤ Review the percentage of time you are allocating to each area.

Consider:

❧ Does this align with getting us to our destination points?

❧ Are there areas that I am completely ignoring?

❧ Are there areas taking too much of my time for the anticipated return?

Don't let daily distractions pull you away completely from what is truly most critical. Set aside some amount of time each day to work on some aspect of implementation. It might be researching to see what changes could affect your business or require you to adjust your plan. It could be looking for evidence to measure how well you are living your values or operating principles. It might be providing feedback and coaching to your direct reports and/or checking in with them on how they are doing, providing positive and realigning feedback to others.

Unfortunately, no matter how much each of us wants to change it, there are only so many hours in the day and so many days in the week. Deciding what we will *not* do is as important and perhaps even more important today than it has ever been. There is so much competing for our time and attention, and much of it is a diversion.

Creating your strategic plan is the easiest part of the job. It is the ongoing execution, including adjusting, that differentiates great leaders and managers today. Sometimes these critical tasks are not as obviously urgent, but, when you are able to pause and really consider their significance to success, it should be evident how important it is for leaders and managers to focus on both the immediate tasks as well as the longer-term destination.

Leaders of the past were often thought of as the only ones involved in strategy. Today, all employees have a role in strategy. Leaders and managers must be able to respond strategically as well as involve themselves in the hands-on implementation of plans. There are few leaders and managers today who purely focus on contemplating the future. It is the day-to-day actions, including communicating, providing feedback, realigning behaviors, and recognizing others, *coupled with* the strategic thinking and doing that equates to success today.

What Remains...What Evolves

Certain aspects of leading and managing that were important 25 years are still critical today, and likely will still be important 100 years from now. These include acting with integrity, leading by example, developing talent, and ensuring customer satisfaction.

There are vast differences between the old-style of administrating and directing, and the new idea of guiding and inspiring. Today's managers and leaders are faced with a whole new set of expectations in the way they motivate the people who work with or follow them, setting the tone for most other aspects of what they do. People today not only don't want to be managed, in most cases, they simply won't be managed. Today's employee wants to be led. They want to participate and engage in every aspect of their jobs. Creating a two-way relationship is critical, especially considering that many knowledgeable workers today know more about what they are doing than their bosses do.

Another significant shift for managers and leaders today is the necessity of thinking globally. The impact of globalization has affected all aspects of business. Appreciating and leveraging diversity is an additional shift that correlates to our world becoming smaller and smaller; the broad expansion of businesses spans seas, cultures, and religions. In addition to these actions and areas of focus, leaders and managers today must be more innovative and more proactive, anticipating problems and opportunities as well as entirely new markets and products.

The days of the exclusively reactive leader and manager are over, with only those who can anticipate emerging trends and deal with constant change able to succeed. Today's leaders and managers can no longer afford to neglect any stakeholder group, and must keep in mind all players—from customers to employees to corporate citizens to suppliers. Developing a new generation of leaders and managers is more of a priority today as well. With a shrinking workforce, it is critically important to have the right people working as productively as possible.

There are few clear career progressions in most companies today, and, if there were, many of today's employees would not be interested in a step-by-step guide to what job to do in what order. Today's employees want options and ongoing development, versus lengthy management courses and specific career paths.

The chart on page 217 captures the changes that are both occurring and necessary.

How About You? Your Own Progress

To keep yourself up to date and developing at the speed of change today, think about and plan how you will keep up, constantly adapt, and learn new ways of being successful. Remember, the more successful you are, the less likely you are to want to change. This is the underlying reason so many

Area	25 Years Ago	Today
Environment	Stability	Constant change
Focus	Managing work	Managing results AND leading people
Thinking horizon	Short term	Short term AND long term
Approach to work	Plans details	Sets direction and monitors
	Fine tuning what is	Creating entirely new/what could be
	Transactional	Transformational
Decision-making	Made them	Facilitates them
	Reactive	Proactive
Energy	Controlling others	Passion for the work, the company, the industry, and the people
Risk-taking	Avoided it	Takes it and enables others to take it
Rules	Made them and measured to them	Breaks them and encourages others to do the same
Conflict	Avoided it	Uses it
Concerned with	Being right	Doing what is right

people keep doing what they have always done, even when they see it is not working or everything else has changed. It is harder to do things differently when we have done well in the past. We rely on our old habits and our comfortable approaches to continue to serve us well. But everything around us is changing, and the way you used to do it may not have relevance in this new environment.

Focus on continual learning **and** unlearning. There are almost no jobs left that will remain the same over time and the demands of leaders and managers are continuing to evolve. The really great ones are constantly learning and developing themselves and they have the following characteristics in common. They:

➤ Like to master things.

> ❖ They are motivated and driven to constantly get better, knowing full well that they will not, and should not, be perfect.

➤ Are observant and flexible.

> ❖ They can consider multiple perspectives to create general guidelines that help them make sense of what is around them.

➤ Focus on problem-solving.

> ❖ They consider current issues from the perspective of making things better versus blaming or worrying.

> ❖ Their thinking is characterized by a balance of the ability to visualize what might or could be, and an effective day-to-day approach to get the right things done.

➤ Are self-aware.

> ❖ They are constantly working to become even more aware of their own intentions as well as their impact on others.

> ❖ They admit mistakes and learn from them.

➤ Are specific, direct, and candid with others.

    ❧ They expose any agenda they have and use good listening skills to really hear what others have to say rather than simply planning their next response.

➤ Have a broad range of interests.

    ❧ They are genuinely curious about others.

    ❧ They are able to make comparisons easily while seeing and appreciating the complexity in the world.

➤ Think strategically.

    ❧ They are able to see, understand, and appreciate the current state as well as see possibilities.

    ❧ When dealing with today's issues, they operate from a broad, long-term perspective rather than taking a narrow view or focusing only on short-term implications.

    ❧ They are able to gather information and make decisions in a timely manner.

➤ Are action-oriented.

    ❧ They get things done.

Leverage what is going on around you all the time for learning. One thing you are almost always involved in as a leader or manager is conversation. The key to conducting a conversation that generates mutual learning and leads to desired outcomes is to ask yourself:

    ❧ Am I willing to be influenced?

    ❧ Am I genuinely interested in what the other person(s) has to say?

    ❧ Do I believe we can learn together?

    ❧ Am I open to learning?

    ❧ When advancing a position, do I reveal the data and reasoning that led to this position?

❧ Do I invite others to test my assumptions?

❧ When faced with another's view with which I disagree, do I ask, "What is it that leads me to my view?"

Your Personal Quarterly Progress Scorecard

Every quarter, ask yourself questions that will help you identify how you did compared to your own personal destination of leading and managing with excellence. Consider what you learned and how to use it in the future.

What should you ask?

The short view: What can I learn from my experiences during the past quarter?

❧ What worked as far as my behaviors, how I stayed focused, and how much progress I made toward my destination? Why?

❧ What didn't work and why?

❧ Knowing what I know now, what could I have done differently?

❧ Which of my assumptions or thought bubbles do I need to challenge or change?

❧ How did I overcome any barriers?

The long view: What are the patterns and trends I have noticed?

❧ How do my current competency, skill, or knowledge levels compare with what they were three months ago? One year ago?

❧ How are my abilities helping me get to my destination?

- Am I enjoying the journey?
- What progress over the last year or so can I feel good about?
- Which challenges keep arising?
- What bubbles are in place about these challenges, and what underlying beliefs do I need to shift if I really want the challenges to dissolve?

The context: How are my actions related to factors in the environment?

- What is around me (such as tools, people, and processes) that is helping me be my best?
- What people or situations do I handle best?
- Who are the people or situations that are a particular challenge?

    If I changed my thought bubbles about them, would it help?

- What are the common elements among those people or situations?
- What can I do differently in the future? Am I willing?

How should you keep track of your own progress?

Keep a notebook that will serve as your learning journal. It does not have to be fancy. It might just be a file folder that you stuff with notes written on napkins. A profoundly valuable development tool, writing down your learning in some sort of organized fashion helps you keep perspective, remember your lessons, and demonstrate your progress.

- Keep it brief. If it's long and detailed, you are less likely to keep it up.

❧ Make it personally meaningful. This is your record, and it doesn't have to follow someone else's formula.

❧ Have fun with it. Don't make it cumbersome.

❧ Note your own accomplishments. What did you write on your own "What's Great?" board?

❧ Track the most important lessons. For example, you might keep a running list of the 10 most important things that you need to remember to remain focused or a list of your prioritized competencies, skills, and knowledge areas.

Learn from success

What better opportunity to learn what works than success? We naturally form behavior patterns very quickly, so look closely at your successes. Rarely do people give success sufficient scrutiny. Success can blind you with glory or lull you because the challenge has passed. In either case, you forgo the inspection that reveals what worked and why.

Be honest with yourself. Determine exactly what you did to succeed.

❧ How much of this success was due to your own actions?

❧ What did you do particularly well?

❧ What did you do that was more effective than what you have done before?

❧ How did you overcome the barriers to doing this?

❧ What could have gone wrong that you managed to avoid?

Transfer the learning. Apply your lessons in other situations.

- ❧ What is your next opportunity to try this?

- ❧ Are there different situations where you could apply what you have learned?

- ❧ What could you do differently that would make this easier next time?

- ❧ How can you improve your performance even more next time?

Find the hidden lesson. Stay open and alert to unexpected learning. Assume that everything you do is a learning opportunity, but that the lesson may not be the one that you want or intend to learn. Most learning takes place on the job, in the day-to-day experiences we have at work. Cultivate your curiosity to constantly consider the development that is often hidden inside your daily experiences.

Learn from mistakes

You won't learn much if blame prevents you from looking at yourself when things go wrong. You also won't learn much if you ignore or conceal mistakes. Instead, you could try to understand what happened and learn from it. Start by figuring out what went wrong. There are no failures when a valuable lesson comes out of it. Learn from others' mistakes as well. You do not have time to make them all yourself!

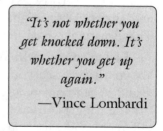

"It's not whether you get knocked down. It's whether you get up again."

—Vince Lombardi

Dust yourself off. No one is perfect. No one wins all the time. Constant learners are resilient. They know that, when they push themselves to the edge, they are bound to fall every now and then, but they do not hesitate to get up and keep going.

Examine the context. Some efforts will fail due to factors outside your control. Consider the entire context to help you determine what is realistically in your control and what is not.

➤ What factors were outside your control? Be objective so you do not avoid responsibility where it truly applies.

➤ How can you anticipate complicating factors in the future and work around or mitigate them in some other way?

➤ How can you influence these factors so they don't get in the way?

    ❧ Did you prepare and practice enough?

    ❧ Did you draw on the resources and people who could help?

    ❧ Did you set realistic goals and expectations?

➤ What do you need to learn before you try this again?

Learn from your emotions

When you start to examine yourself, you may experience frustration, surprise, satisfaction, relief, apprehension, guilt, and anxiety. You might even experience all of these at once! This is natural, so do not get too concerned.

Listen to yourself. When you are happy or content, think about what caused your success and how you can achieve it again. When you are angry, frustrated, or embarrassed, identify the triggers. Then figure out how you can think about it differently and what you can do differently the next time. Keep in mind that it is not usually the actual event, situation, or person that created the feelings you are having, it is the meaning you have attached to it that created those feelings.

Stick with it. One problem with reflection is that it doesn't always feel good. But paying attention to your feelings now can help you prevent frustration in the future. Just like physical pain, negative emotions draw your attention to something that isn't the way it should be. Use your emotional pain to:

- ❧ Take initiative. Discomfort can be a motivator for change.

- ❧ Draw your attention to something you may be ignoring. Don't let emotions prevent you from examining the situation openly and objectively, including your own thought bubbles.

- ❧ Identify areas of future growth. If the pain isn't related to a current priority for your development, make a note so you can think about it next time you consider your destination and plan your action steps to get there.

Coping With Barriers

Each step in developing presents its own challenges. Once again, you need to honestly appraise what gets in your way of pausing to consider, reflect, and refocus. Today's pace gets in the way of growth. We take care of the e-mails and urgent requests, but we lose focus on moving ourselves forward. You have to form deeply held beliefs about the power of your own development before you will shift your behaviors. Take the time to consider what is really important to you and how strongly you feel about achieving it. Now consider what you must believe to achieve these goals. When your underlying beliefs support getting you to your destination, you will be amazed at how the rest of you moves towards the target. Our underlying beliefs are what drive our behaviors, so work on those first and then measure your actions. A few other tips to progress on your own development:

- ❧ Constantly assess the payback to you and how the development supports getting you to where you want to go.

❧ Enlist others to support your change and to hold you accountable. Ask for their help and assistance. Almost everyone likes to help others when asked.

❧ Recognize that change requires time and practice before it becomes natural. It also proceeds in fits and starts, sometimes moving two steps forward, then one step back. Your changes will occur only with persistence and practice.

Focus on New Goals

You have now completed a full cycle. It is time to apply your new knowledge and skills to the next three months.

> There is always more to develop. Keep learning!

With each cycle, the process becomes easier and more natural. You experience rewards from your efforts and risk-taking. As others see you grow, they give you new opportunities. It becomes a virtuous cycle of growth and development.

Just as you measure progress for the organization, you must audit your own progress as well. Your current circumstances, opportunities, and capabilities should look different from when you started and you should be moving closer to your personal destination. Recognize and value your progress. Think about what you can do now that you could not do before?

How About the Organization? Making It *the Way Things Are Done Here*

To focus the whole organization on this same type of learning, consider the systems, tools, processes, and expectations for individual development. Once individual development is being role-modeled by leaders and managers, it makes sense to embed it as an organization-wide practice. But do not try to launch a development program until you are ready to do it yourself!

Leader and manager development tips

The following are tips on actions you can take to constantly improve development within your organization:

> ➤ Regularly ask for specific feedback from different perspectives—your manager, peers, customers, clients, and direct reports. Get data and examples.

> ➤ Frequently check in with people you respect and trust, and ask how you are doing in those areas important for your development.

> ➤ Find a development partner—someone who will help hold you accountable to developing in those areas you have targeted.

> ➤ Make development one of your management practices. Schedule it and include it on your to-do list or whatever mechanism you use to focus your time and attention.

> ➤ Find out and understand the other person's interests and motivation, and help plan development around both your needs and theirs.

> ➤ Encourage employees to ask questions and challenge things that do not make sense to them. "Why are we doing this?" "Why are we doing it this way?" "Why aren't we doing it this way?" "How can we...?" These are all great questions that you should encourage employees to ask and learn.

> ➤ Make time to have development-focused conversations.

> ➤ Expect employees to find development opportunities. Ask them what they learned in the last month. Provide suggestions to get them started.

➤ At year-end, ask employees how they have grown over the year and what they want to focus on for the next year.

➤ Listen attentively.

> ❧ Do not interrupt or spend your listening time planning what you will say when the person is finished.

> ❧ Restate what you believe the other person said and wait for his or her feedback on your interpretation. Understand the speaker's point of view before responding with yours.

> ❧ Ask questions to gather more information, allowing you to better understand the other person's ideas and motivators. Do not pose the questions in a demeaning way so as to intimidate the other person.

➤ Take note of accomplishments and effective behavior as soon as it occurs, and express appreciation and recognition quickly. This immediate feedback is the most effective way to reinforce the desired behavior. It also aids in the accumulation of specific examples for performance reviews.

➤ Ask for input on projects and issues. This will stretch the abilities of others and will promote ownership and a feeling of contribution.

➤ Stay connected. Walk the halls to keep up to date on individuals so you can relate to what is current for them.

➤ Consider what procedures or practices are in place to establish a "safe haven" for employees to notify you that they are overloaded or stressed. What actions are taken once you are informed?

➤ Help people identify the connection between their ongoing learning and development, and the impact it has on the organization, the department, and the team.

➤ Provide prompt, continual, constructive feedback to improve performance, focusing on what to do differently in the future.

➤ Focus on specific behaviors and not on personality. Identify specific details on the gap between expected and actual performance and how it affects the project, the organization, the team, and the customers. Provide ideas on how to do things differently so the employee can develop in ways that meet your expectations.

➤ Reward out-of-the-box thinking and risk-taking. Encourage others to value their mistakes as a learning opportunity and normal part of the process of developing. Communicate that perfectionism hinders risk-taking.

➤ Work with each staff member to identify his or her strengths and weaknesses. Discuss how to leverage strengths and minimize weaknesses while adding value to the business.

➤ Set incremental development goals and action plans (quarterly, annually) for all staff members and get their input for continuous improvement. Focus on their career development and not just their performance within their current role.

➤ Encourage staff members to share their learning and how it can be applied to other processes and projects. By sharing *what* worked well and what could be changed, the process, including the *how* it got done rather than exclusively the result, becomes the focus.

➤ Encourage risk-taking within defined boundaries to develop employees' ability to think and act outside their comfort zones. Help people see failure as a learning experience. Support them and help them maintain self-esteem.

➤ Know the skill set and competencies of your team members. Assign responsibility and authority accordingly and be patient with their growth and "bumps in the road."

In Conclusion

If you have gotten through all this material and begun to apply some of the practices outlined, you are definitely spending more than a minute to be a truly effective leader or manager!

Use this book as a reference tool to refresh yourself every now and then. Keep it in front of you to drive your focus. Discuss the concepts and action items presented with others. Practice using the checklists and outlines provided. The more it stays on your radar, the more likely you are to use it to drive success in your organization and for yourself.

And, in 25 years, we will be writing about you!

Chapter 5 Executables

➤ What gets measured gets done.

- Regularly track progress against performance goals and objectives as a means to recognize and reward employees who contribute to getting you to your destination.

- Use your breakthrough model for creating an ongoing tracking and measurement system.

- Measure against standards of excellence and the desired state. What does the desired state look when you get there? What do the desired behaviors look like?

➤ What are the significant projects or initiatives that must occur to move you from your current state to your desired state?

- Focus on only three to five strategies. Too many and you become unfocused. Too few and your day-to-day activities will support no strategy at all.

➤ Create your own "Plate Exercise."

  ❧ What is on the plate and what should fall off?

  ❧ What should you start, stop, and continue doing to keep your efforts focused on the highest value activities?

➤ Clarify your strategy and goals, and manage alignment across individuals, departments, and initiatives using a scorecard.

➤ Embrace the idea of continuous learning. Look for it in all that you do, including leveraging and asking yourself observant questions about your interactions with, and reactions to, people and situations.

➤ Learn to appreciate your mistakes. They are inevitable. They make you human, humble, and grateful!

Index

About the Author

HOLLY G. GREEN is currently the CEO and managing director of The Human Factor, Inc. She has more than 20 years of executive level and operations experience in *Fortune* 500, entrepreneurial, and management consulting organizations, including The Coca-Cola Company, AT&T, Dell Computer, Bass Hotels & Resorts, Expedia, Inc., RealNetworks, Inc., Microsoft and Google. She was previously president of The Ken Blanchard Companies, a global consulting and training organization as well as LumMed, Inc., a biotech start-up. She has a broad background in strategic planning, organization design and development, process improvement, and leadership assessment and development.

With a proven track record of value-added delivery and as a sought-after speaker and consultant, she has received national recognition.

Holly lives in San Diego, California, with her husband, two children, and two dogs.

Visit *www.MoreThanAMinute.com* to stay up to date on being a great leader and manager today.

Also Available From Career Press

100 Ways to Motivate Yourself
978-1-56414-775-2

Financial Statements, Revised Edition
978-1-56414-023-0

100 Ways to Motivate Others
978-1-56414-992-3

How to Win Any Argument
978-1-56414-810-0

6 Habits of Highly Effective Teams
978-1-56414-972-5

Ask the Right Questions, Hire the Best People,
2nd Edition
978-1-56414-892-6

Capitalizing on Kindness
978-1-60163-038-4

Business Letters for Busy People, 4th Edition
978-1-56414-612-0